HOW
I MADE
$500,000
in selling at age 69

GOPI NAIR
Gratitude Practitioner

Auctorem House
276 5th Ave, Ste 704-2591
New York, NY 10001
www.auctoremhouse.com
1.888.332.7718

Contents

CHAPTER ONE

What You See Is What You Get

The year was 1980, and I was shopping for men's shirts in the Sears store in Oak Brook, Illinois. The men's store was filled with plenty of shirts, but I could not find one in my neck size. I asked the young salesgirl, "Ma'am, do you have a 14 ½ size in this pattern?" She looked at me, smiled, and said, "Sir, what you see is what you get."

Despite the hint of dismay in my heart, I felt an inner jolt; this salesgirl was revealing a secret of accomplishment to me, although she was not aware of it herself. In our everyday life, our experience of external events and conditions is determined by our internal perspective. We are constantly attracting events that manifest by sending our own thoughts which weave those events for us. Every manifested event is the outcome of the thoughts that we secretly entertain in the mind; most of us do not know that we are actually the authors of our own book of experience.

The $500,000 Sales Goal

At the beginning of 2012, I set my sales goal at $500,000, just as I do every year. First, I wrote it down on a piece of paper, and then wrote it down on my kitchen board where I can see it first thing in the morning. The kitchen table is where I go to begin my day; there, I allow my spirit to dwell on my aspirations.

I used a bright green marker to write down my goal in order to clearly see that number, even when the lights are off. My wife and children might have seen that number, but nobody has asked me about its significance—they all know that I am little unconventional about my mind management practice. I do this because I know that one of the principles of goal setting is that the goal should be in writing; ideally, one should be able to look at it and internalize it several times a day on a casual basis, especially during the semi-waking hours. This assists in the process of positive visualization.

Positive Visualization

The human mind is constantly engaged in visualization, very often imagining negative scenarios and projecting drama onto the screen of our mind. This process continues throughout our waking and sleeping hours; what we call dreams or nightmares are nothing but our thoughts manifesting as visualizations. If we carefully analyze even our worst nightmares, we can trace them back to fearful thoughts that we have consciously or unconsciously entertained. Since we all visualize on a regular basis, we can easily cultivate the habit of positive visualizations. It amounts to retraining our mind, like learning to flip a coin to deliberately get the head side instead of the tail side. With a focused intent, anyone can perform positive visualizations.

The Scientific Basis

The seat of visualization is in the power of imagination—and imagination is the most God-like quality in man. Imagination comes naturally to small children, and they can create any role they want to play as they "make believe." Sadly, this precious God-like quality is often lost as children grow into adults.

Many of us go through life imagining lack, limitation, and ill health—and we create these scenarios. After creating those painful experiences, we engage in a blame game, blaming our parents and our education (or lack of it) for our shortcomings. We are the authors of our own lack and limitations; if we simply shift our imagination from negative to positive, we can radically change our experiences for the better.

The following exercise will help every person engaged in sales to get a handle on positive visualization:

Sl. No.	Name of the Prospect	Loan Amt	Remarks
1.	Patrick Murphy*	$250,000	Left message
2.	Joan Sandler	300,000	Gave a quote
3.	Eileen McNamara	200,000	Emailed GFE
4.	Rajesh Patel	300,000	Emailed GFE
5.	Edward Salazar	200,000	Sent appl.
6.	Manish Arora	500,000	Met first time
7.	Laila Hasan	350,000	Sent pre approval
8.	Joseph Abraham	180,000	Sent pre approval
9.	Peter Batsman	400,000	Emailed appl.
10.	Rosa Parekh	250,000	Emailed appl.

Every day, before your day starts, look at your M. Sales Target and make changes to the sales cycle.

Sales Cycle

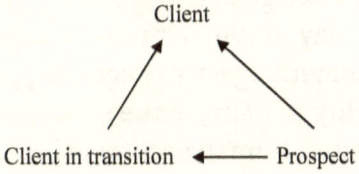

Client

Client in transition ◄——— Prospect

---

*   A list of my prospects (not real name) who enquired about mort-gages

Who is a Prospect?

1. A person who showed some interest A person whom you called A person whose referral you got from a client person whose name is on a list you bought Anyone you consider a prospect

Who is a Client in Transit?

1. A prospect whom you contacted, by telephone, letter, email, or in person
2. A prospect to whom you sent an application
3. A person to whom you sent a GFE
4. A person to whom you sent any information
5. A person who contacted you by any means of communication

Who is a Client?

1. A client in transit who finalized the transaction with you
2. A client in transit whom you could not close due to financial difficulties
3. A client in transit who withdrew the application for whatever reason
4. A client in transit who could not qualify for the product this time

As sales professionals, our goal is to convert every prospect into a client while continuing to serve them. Once we have written down our monthly sales goal, and when we have looked at these sales goals every day (several times a day) while recording changes, there is something very special happening in our mind. We are, in fact, trying to impress the subconscious mind, which is the power behind all human accomplishments. Once the subconscious mind is impressed, it will transcend time and space to manifest our desires into their physical equivalents. Thus our goals become our physical reality.

The magic of manifestation is hidden in the power of the subconscious mind, which is an obedient servant of the conscious mind—the Master Mind. This is the truth every sales person must recognize early in his sales training to become highly successful. While education and training help us in our accomplishments, the key to greater sales success lies in understanding and tapping the power of the subconscious mind. You may not gain mastery over the subconscious mind in the beginning, but with perseverance, anybody can reach goals beyond one's wildest dreams.

Don'ts in Sales Planning

1. Don't dwell on your shortcomings; this will impede your success.
2. Don't think about the logic behind the success; there is no logic.
3. Don't think that your goal has to manifest in certain ways; if you do this, you are erecting your own walls of resistance which will definitely bring negative results.
4. Don't discuss your sales goals with anybody, as there will often be "Doubting Thomases" around you. They can dampen your enthusiasm with their negative feedback.
5. Don't compare yourself with anybody else in your organization; you are not trying to compete with them.
6. Don't boast about your accomplishments; your inflated ego can halt your progress.
7. Don't complain about anything during this process; simply trust the Universe and remain grateful.

The Role of Positive Visualization in Sales

The role of positive visualization in the field of selling can not be overemphasized, as emotionally-charged positive visualization induces self-hypnosis. Please note that the term *self-hypnosis* need not intimidate you, because we all engage in self-hypnosis, mostly in a negative fashion. We constantly think of things we do not want, such as lack, limitation, and sickness. Do not think, talk, or do anything that stimulates negativity; as the Buddha, the enlightened one, said, "You become what you think all day long."

When we constantly think about any one thing, we are using our conscious mind, which is our thinking mind; that information seeps into our subconscious mind, which accepts it "as is." The subconscious mind can be compared as the soil which simply accepts whatever seed the farmer chooses to sow, without questioning its use or uselessness. Deductive reasoning is the true nature of the subconscious mind, and it accepts whatever the conscious mind gives; then, it acts to produce its manifestation. Since the subconscious mind transcends time and space, it has unlimited power to attract the resources necessary to manifest whatever desires you impress upon it.

How to Command the Subconscious Mind

We say that we do not know how to command the subconscious mind, yet we are all doing it every day. The commands we unconsciously give are often negative, manifesting negative results. We can reverse this process by consciously and deliberately commanding the subconscious mind. The commanding tool that we use to program the subconscious mind is called *positive affirmation*. Every affirmation, when recited with emotion at certain times, will be accepted by the subconscious mind; in time, their manifestation becomes certain, just like a seed sprouts after it is sown in the fertile soil. All the resources required for the manifestation of our desires are attracted by the subconscious mind from far and near as it transcends time and space.

Two Sales Affirmations

1. I AM GRATEFUL FOR MY SALES
2. EVERY DAY, IN EVERY WAY MY SALES ARE INCREASING.

Write down these affirmations on a 3x5 card. Recite these affirmations several times a day—particularly as soon as you wake up in the morning, and just before slipping into sleep, as these semi-waking hours are when the conscious mind is most receptive to your command.

No Logic in Success

There is absolutely no logic in success; there is simply emotion. Any emotionally-charged affirmation will manifest itself, regardless of who you are, what your educational background is, or which race or religion you belong to. Our logical mind is the conscious mind, the master mind, the arguing mind, the goal-setting mind, the commander-in-chief who is ready to give command to the subconscious mind. The subconscious mind is the loyal servant, ready to take orders from the master, whatever they may be, carrying them out with cunning accuracy. The problem with most of us is that we give conflicting commands to the subconscious mind; this causes confusion, and as a result, nothing happens. Therefore, we must use affirmations, ideally at the prescribed times: dawn, dusk, or any semi-waking hours when the conscious mind is in a state of abeyance. If you notice, these are the times prescribed by most religions for prayers, which are, in essence, positive affirmations; our ancestors knew the mode of operations for the human mind.

My $500,000 Goal

When I wrote my goal, I encountered many doubts about my ability to achieve it; this is only natural. In my particular case, age is an issue. *Will I have enough stamina to achieve my goal?* I asked myself. My past performance was nowhere near my goal. Whenever those doubts arose in my mind, I recited the following affirmation:

"I AM GRATEFUL FOR THIS EXPERIENCE."

Gratitude erases all negativity from the shores of human mind. It removes all our ailments and suffering. It is a cure for all our pains, both physical and mental. A mind that is filled with gratitude alone can invoke more blessings from the Universe. This Universe is a very kind place. It simply returns what you give—but manyfold. The farmer knows this the best: he sows a seed, and reaps many times.

An ungrateful salesman will dig his own hole of failure and frustration. Choose to appreciate everything around you. It will energize you, it can stimulate positive thinking in you. Remain grateful to all prospects clients, regardless of how they treat you. They will pick up those vibrations of gratitude, and they will respond in kind. Most of the time, the opposite happens; we complain, think ill of our prospects, and they never become our clients, because they picked up your ungrateful vibration.

Carry Your Own Sunshine

Once upon a time, certain creatures complained to the Sun.

"There is a location in Universe immersed in thick darkness," they said. "It is a horrifying sight, invoking fear in everyone who sees it."

"I have never heard about such a place," answered the Sun. "If there is such a place, I ought to visit it!"

Followed by these creatures, the Sun set out to see the darkest spot in the Universe. As the Sun reached this place, all darkness disappeared.

We as salespeople must carry our own sunshine wherever we go. When unfriendly or doubting prospects feel the warmth of our hearts, they too will become our clients. As St. Francis of Assisi said, "It is in giving that we receive." Therefore, we must profusely give our love, compassion, care, and undivided attention to all those whom we choose to serve.

Watch Your Thoughts

We must constantly watch our thoughts. Anytime any doubts or a negative thought arises, do not dwell on it. Instead, divert the attention to your Sales Affirmations. If necessary, verbally recite the affirmations ten times until the negativity disappears. If negativity returns, do the same thing over and over until your mind is calm. A calm and relaxed mind is a creative mind. Only a creative mind can lead you to every kind of accomplishments in any field of human endeavor. A conscious effort on the part of every salesperson to watch his or her thoughts is a prerequisite for focused behavior. When you focus on any object of desire, you are bringing your own thought energy without distractions, thus your thoughts are available to create a powerful spiritual prototype of your desire. These powerful spiritual prototypes, with continued efforts in concentration, will translate themselves into their physical equivalents. The following chart will explain the process of creation in an individual:

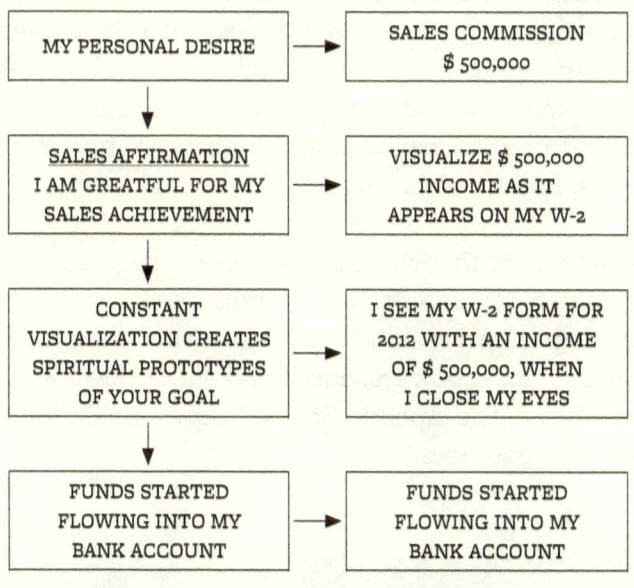

The above chart itself is an eye-opener to the internal process of every human achievement. It all begins with the power of desire. There is an all-consuming fire in the power of desire; it is more powerful than a raging wildfire. It burns away all obstacles on the way to the manifestation of our desire. When you diligently follow the process, physical manifestation is only a matter of time; you keep yourself busy doing everything on a daily basis without casting any shadow of doubt. Whenever doubts creep up, as they are bound to, repeat the process without dwelling on the doubts.

We are logical thinkers—but there is no logic in human accomplishments, only emotion. The subconscious mind is all-powerful, invincible, and is the seat of all emotions. By invoking the power of the subconscious mind, you can translate even your outlandish dreams into physical reality.

Most of the time, we are prisoners of our own limited knowledge, which creates barriers in reaching our true potential. While it is necessary for us to have an education that helps us to think logically, we need to expand our logical thinking to the realm of the unknown, where the subconscious mind dwells. Use your logical mind as a "master mind" to tap into the power of the subconscious mind, which transcends time and space. It will unleash its spiritual tentacles to attract and gather resources from far and near to translate any dream, no matter how outlandish it is, into its physical reality.

Our only enemy in the whole process of accomplishment is our doubt. Negative thinking causes doubt. The only effective tool in combating negative thinking is *gratitude*—a grateful attitude. It has magical powers, and it can shoot down all negative thoughts—hence the Apostle St. Paul proclaimed, "Be grateful under all circumstances."

Keep Your Score

Every salesperson must keep his score. The old saying "Don't expect what you don't inspect" is absolutely true. Personally, I am very passionate about keeping score. Almost every day, I sit at my kitchen table with a cup of tea and write down my sales performance for every month. There is a science behind keeping score. When you write down your accomplishments, you are putting on notice the subconscious mind that you are doing great. That success vibration is picked up by the subconscious mind, who in turn will sustain that flow of success. Hence the expression, "Nothing succeeds like success." Every time you succeed in making a sale, and you write it down and look at the number with gratitude, it goes into the memory bank of the subconscious mind. As you know, subconscious mind is the seat of memory, and all your feelings of success are stored therein.

Your Memory Bank

MEMORY BANK

October	November	December
July	August	September
April	May	June
January	February	March

Every time you make a sale, it should be deposited in your Memory Bank with a note of gratitude. The very act of depositing your feeling of success with a note of gratitude has spiritual connotations. You are indeed impregnating the subconscious mind, which is your memory keeper. Every time you attempt to make a sale, your memory of success stimulates your presentation with inspiration and confidence, and more success will come. This is the secret behind successful salespeople becoming more successful as they are able to close most of their clients. The clients themselves will feel the success of the salesperson, and they become impressed with him. The result is consummation of the sale. It is also a fact of life that the whole world wants to dance around those who are successful and prosperous. Who wants to dance around losers, anyway?

My Sales Memory Bank

2012 (Actual Numbers)

January	February	March
19329	28049	34262

2012

April	May	June
33126	25025	27711

2012

July	August	September
27354	24544	31414

2012

October	November	December
25464	24965	213722

If you look at the sale accomplishments in each quarter, it was not proportionate to my goal. I should have shown $125,000.00 every quarter to be on target for my goal. But it did not happen. I did not worry about it because the subconscious mind does not want to be micromanaged. If your goal is deeply impressed upon the subconscious mind, it will move earth and heaven to make it happen. If I become restless and dictate that the goal should be accomplished in a certain way, I am erecting a wall of resistance, and my goal will not be accomplished. It also shows that I do not trust the power of the subconscious to carry out my command. Instead of worrying about the accomplishment of goal, I simply stay the course, doing what I am supposed to do in my daily sales life. We are human beings, and occasionally doubts will creep into our consciousness; at that time do not resist it. Instead, recite your mantra:

"I am grateful for the lesson."

The lesson is to trust your subconscious mind, and let it do its job. Simply relax, and get yourself busy with daily sales chores. We must have the faith of a farmer. He sows the seeds, waters the soil, and makes sure it is exposed to enough sunlight. As the seed sprouts, he adds whatever manure is required for the healthy plants, which ensures a bountiful harvest. The farmer does not pull the seed daily to find out if it is sprouting. He knows, and he simply obeys the law of nature.

We salespeople must learn from the farmer's example; we must entrust our goal to the obeying mind, and let it work it out. We patiently wait while we are engaged in the day-to-day sales activities of prospecting, giving presentations, and facilitating closings.

Regardless of where you are in sales numbers at the end of any quarter, your goal will be an accomplished reality by the end of the last day of the year. Many successful salespeople have confided in me that they too had similar experiences; the goal became an accomplished fact, and many seemingly impossible events loomed on the horizon to make their dreams come true. All these experiences point out that the invincible and inexplicable power of the subconscious cannot be underestimated. The conscious mind simply has to give the command to the subjective mind; there should be no doubt about the capacity of the subconscious mind to carry out the order given. There is no reason to have any doubt, because the subconscious is an inlet to the universal mind, the ultimate source of all the resources where there is no lack or limitation. The only limitation we have is a limitation that we impose, either knowingly or unknowingly.

Any time things are not going well, there are two things you must do to keep yourself busy:

Make more "cold calls" or send e-mails about your products or services: Bearing in mind that the expression "cold call" is a misnomer—you can make every call a "warm call" by putting in your warmth and emotion—earnestly present your case, always keeping in mind the best interest of the prospective client.

Remember, one must not indulge in any sales activity with the sole intention of making a commission for oneself; this intention cuts down the very root of sales integrity. We are all in the service business and are part of a problem-solving enterprise; we help our customers to solve their problems, and in the process, as a byproduct of our service, we get paid. Any business relationship—or any relationship, for that matter—must be built on the premise of mutual benefit and mutual trust, especially if it is to be for the long term.

Appreciate our associates: The second thing we all can do on a regular basis is to validate those who work long hours; they are often underpaid and under-appreciated. Small tokens of appreciation will go a long way in cementing relationships with support staff. Just as a word of appreciation or a thank-you card from clients boosts our morale, the same benefit applies to our support staff when we demonstrate that we appreciate them.

Send thank-you cards, buy flowers and candies, or take them out for lunch on a Friday afternoon. It is not the few dollars that you spend that matter—it's about your willingness to express your gratitude to those who work with you throughout the year. It is indeed a good spiritual practice to appreciate others who support you.

CHAPTER TWO

Gratitude Must Be The Only Attitude

G ratitude must be the only attitude in life. It is a great attitude. We seldom realize that gratitude is the golden key to unlock the door to the power of the subconscious mind. The power of gratitude to inspire positive emotions was known to our ancestors who incorporated the practice of gratitude before the beginning of every type of prayer. The Mayans, the Persians, the Chinese, the Indians, the Egyptians, and the Babylonians all preached gratitude to invoke their gods. The enlightened ones of almost all the cultures around the world knew the power of gratitude in realizing great the human potential that lies beneath the layers of consciousness. The kingdom of Heaven is within, proclaims the New Testament, indicating the great Hall of Harmony that is hidden in every human being, regardless of one's education, gender, creed or race.

A daily practice of gratitude by every salesperson is a guarantee that he or she can keep discouragement at bay in everyday life. Many highly talented and highly trained salespeople fall by the wayside as they are consumed by the raging fires of discouragement, despair, and despondency. Gratitude is a magic wand which can erase the discouragement that stems from negativity, once and for all. Just like the fog vanishes when the sun rises in the morning, all negative thoughts flee when you practice gratitude.

We hear about gratitude in church sermons, while reading scriptures, or from grandma's wisdom. The diligent practice of gratitude can introduce miracles in your life. It can improve:

- Professional life
- Family relationships
- Physical health
- Mental and emotional wellbeing

Why is Gratitude Important in Sales?

Any successful salesperson will know that "selling is a way of life." It is not only a way of material life—it is a part of our spiritual life, too. There are ups and downs, ecstasy and agony, expectation and disappointment, acceptance and rejection. We work long hours, we travel long distances, and it often takes us away from the family for days together. Many times we feel lonely.

Rejection is every salesperson's nightmare, especially in the beginning of one's career. It has ruined the lives of many ambitious young men and women who could have been highly successful had they been trained to handle rejection properly. Knowing the impact of rejection on one's sales career, many employers have incorporated specific training programs to handle rejection.

Gratitude—The Best Tool

Gratitude is the best training tool for handling rejection. When you have appreciation built into your personality, and when your mind is immersed in gratitude, there is no room for negative thinking. The vibrations of gratitude will be felt by your prospective client, and most of the time, you will be accepted rather than rejected. Gratitude opens many doors to a salesperson and acts as a catalyst between you and the customer. It builds a subliminal bridge of trust where you communicate at the deepest level of consciousness, creating good chemistry between you and the customer; they will intuitively feel your sincerity and earnestness.

A Clean Mind, A Healthy Body

A very important prerequisite for any sales career is a clean mind and healthy body. A clean mind is an incubator of your dreams, and a healthy body is merely an instrument of its expression. Those who practice gratitude daily in all aspects of life will have the know-how for a clean mind and healthy body. The mind/body connection, the healing power of gratitude, the origin of any disease, and the scientific discovery in those areas are described in the following pages. The information must be not only read, but must be practiced by every salesperson to harvest total harmony in life. A well-balanced person with a clean mind and healthy body alone can climb the ladder of success in sales. After all, we are the brave people who have willingly exchanged job security for prosperity. That prosperity begins with a prosperous mind and prosperous body.

Practice of Gratitude

I began practicing gratitude as a daily ritual in 2009 after spending hours reading about gratitude in the Bible, Quran, and Bhagavad Geetha. I sought out all the literature I could on the subject of gratitude and simply started the practice; I studied the customs of many cultures around the world to gain insight into the meaning and power of gratitude. When I started practicing gratitude, I began to experience an inexplicable sense of calm while dealing with challenging situations, which ordinarily would wreck anybody's peace of mind. I routinely started saying,

"I am grateful for your business and friendship" when dealing with my clients; every time I used that expression, I poured lots of emotion into the words, which created strong vibrations. The words were not simply coming from my lips—they started flowing from the depth of my being. Many times I experienced teary eyes as I conveyed my heartfelt gratitude to my clients. An ounce of gratitude can lift a ton of pain and suffering, both physical and emotional, in anybody's life.

My Daily Routine

As soon as I open my eyes in the morning, and before getting out of my bed, I take a few minutes for a simple prayer of gratitude. I basically recite the following:

> I am grateful to my Creator.
> I am grateful to my parents.
> I am grateful to my teachers, from whom I learned directly or indirectly.
> I am grateful to my brothers, sisters, and friends who helped shape my life.
> I am grateful to my spouse and children, who give me their love and emotional support.
> I am grateful for another great day in my life.
> I am grateful to my boss, my colleagues at work, and all my prospects and clients.

It only takes a couple of minutes to complete this prayer. This is the best and most effective prayer you will say in your lifetime, and it meets the criteria for effective prayer (listed below):

1. Prayer must be positive (gratitude is the most positive expression of appreciation). Prayer must be recited in the semi-waking hours, when the conscious mind is in a slumbering state (before you get out of bed, you are still in a semi-waking state). Prayer must be acted upon by the

subconscious mind (this is the best time to impress upon the subconscious mind, as it is in a state of peak alert, because the conscious mind is still in a slumbering state).

Every salesperson would be well-served to keep this simple dialogue at the forefront of their mind.

As you know, every thought is a command for the subconscious mind. As soon as the powerful thought is unleashed, the subconscious mind reacts.

Let's assume that I say in the morning that I am grateful for this terrific day. My internal dialogue would then go on as follows:

> "My boss (the conscious mind) thinks that it is a terrific day. Let me make sure that he is right. Since subconscious transcends time and space, it can attract all the resources from far and near to make your desire of a terrific day an awesome reality. The more emotion you pour into your prayer, the more effective a command it will give to the subconscious mind, which does not argue. It simply obeys the master's command, without questioning its validity. Thus your every day becomes a terrific day which will pave your way to greater sales success."

Similarly, I also practice a simple prayer of gratitude just before slipping into deep sleep. It is so simple that it goes like a whisper:

> "I am grateful for another great day."

More than half a century ago, while growing up in a small village in the South Indian state of Kerala, I was intrigued by my mother's extraordinary behavior. My older brother was away working in Northern India, and we used to get mail regularly from him at least once every month. I still remember the mailman:

he used to announce his arrival before he entered the fenced compound; his name was Kesavan Nair, and he was a heavy-set middle-aged man with swollen feet. Mother was always very pleased with him, and I, along with my older sister, would draw near to witness the "event" of Mother receiving the mail and the money order.

After signing for the money order and receiving the letter, my mother would offer the mailman lunch, which was always a custom in our home. After the simple lunch, my mother would give him a gratuity of one rupee. I questioned my mother about giving the gratuity to the mailman every time he delivered the mail. My mother said, "Gopi, you have to be grateful to the mailman, because he brings good news from your brother. A small gratuity is only a token of gratitude."

Even though her answer satisfied my curious mind, I still did not "get it." But one thing I remember: that mailman (or any mailman for that matter) never brought bad news to my mother. This was my first lesson in gratitude.

Origin of the Word *Gratitude*

The English word *gratitude* has its origin in the Latin word "gratus" (which means pleasing) or the French word "gratitudo" (which means thanks). Gratitude simply means a grateful attitude. It also means a deep appreciation for all the blessings you enjoy. In a deeper and spiritual sense, gratitude refers to a spiritual acknowledgment that "all is well." This spiritual assertion in the affirmative is the metaphysical key to understanding the mystical power of gratitude. In that sense, it is an invitation to divine grace to flow into your life.

It is said that a grateful heart is ready to receive more blessings. A daily dose of gratitude provides a heart-healthy diet; it ensures your spiritual wellbeing, regardless of who you are and where you are going.

Saying "Thank You" vs. Gratitude

When one says "thank you," it is usually in acknowledgment of a favor received from another. However, gratitude goes deeper than words: gratitude is a state of mind and a spiritual acknowledgment that "all is well." Gratitude involves people, events and conditions. It acknowledges not only favors or benefits received, it appreciates the experience as beneficial.

A grateful attitude is an all-encompassing state of mind, where tranquility and harmony alone reign. In that mental state, there is the utmost satisfaction; nothing is lacking, because the focus is on the present, and the focus is on the blessings.

While saying "thank you" brings a temporary happy feeling, gratitude grants contentment. When you are in a state of gratitude, you are so busy counting your blessings that there is no reason for discontentment.

Gratitude is the mother of many healing emotions, like love, compassion and forgiveness. Practicing gratitude as a way of life will result in total surrender. Gratitude brings you a life-changing experience. It promotes spiritual wellbeing and teaches you that everything is on purpose, and that there are no accidents in the universe. The ultimate benefit of gratitude is total surrender—surrender to that higher power from where we inherited our spark of divinity.

Gratitude in Scripture and History

In his letter to Thessalonians, St. Paul wrote *en panti eucharisteite* (pronounced IN PAN-TEE UCARSTA-TE) which was translated in The King James version of the Bible as "in everything, give thanks."

Panti is derived from the Greek word *pas* which means *all*. In the context of St. Paul's teachings, *panti* refers to "all circumstances" whether good or bad. *Eucharisteite* is derived from *eucharizes* which could also mean "be grateful." Thus St. Paul was giving the scripture teaching, "be grateful in all circumstances."

In the fourth chapter of Philippians, it is said "Be careful (or anxious) for nothing, but in everything, by prayer and supplications, and with thanksgiving, let your requests be made known with God." Thus the Bible reminds us to remain free from worry and anxiety. With gratitude in our hearts, we pray for God's grace, and our prayers will be answered. In this context, gratitude is a prerequisite for the prayer to be effective, because our focus is on gratitude, which helps us to remove worry and anxiety, whether our prayers will be answered or not.

It is interesting to note the expression "in everything." Everything is possible with prayer and with a grateful attitude. This assurance in the scripture is a guarantee of the metaphysical truth "ask and you shall receive, seek and you shall find, knock and it shall be opened unto you." By emphasizing gratitude, asking becomes very effective, as there is no trace of fear or worry about the outcome.

According to Bhagavad Geetha, a sacred text of the Hindus, one is urged to do one's duty in a spirit of gratitude without any expectation of a reward. At the same time, through the operation of the Law of Karma, the exact reward will be given for the quality of work accomplished. The Law of Karma, simply put, only means that you cannot reap apples if you sowed the seeds of oranges. It is similar to the theory of sowing and reaping as explained in the Bible. The Hindu scripture also reminds us not to expect any gratitude for good deeds that we do for others. This reminder is to help us focus on the task at hand, and not to get disappointed if our expectation of gratitude does not materialize.

In Peru, the people celebrate an offering of gratitude called the Peruvian Ayni Despacho. All the material things that are offered at this ceremony represent gratitude to Mother Earth and other forces of nature. Peruvians respectfully remember Pachamama, who is considered the provider of all our needs for physical existence. The entire ceremony is based on psychic awareness; after the ceremony, the participants not only feel a sense of external contentment—they become more aware of the need to be grateful for all the forces of nature.

The constitution of the fourteenth century Native American Iroquois begins with a prayer of gratitude. It offers its expression of gratitude "...to the earth where men dwell, to streams of water, springs and lakes; to the maize and fruits and medicinal herbs; to the sun, moon and the thunder; and to the great creator, the source of all life." What a magnificent way to begin a constitution; it provides the framework of a code of conduct for an ancient tribe.

A grateful attitude is basically an expression of a delight of gratitude, to people, places and events that help shape our lives. Thus we are all indebted to our God the creator, and to our parents who gave birth and raised us to become mature and responsible adults.

It is a custom in many cultures to offer grace before a meal, to express gratitude to the forces of nature, to the fertile lands, to the farmers who grow the crops, and the shopkeepers who make them available to us for consumption. Also, when food is digested properly, our internal digestive system itself is revitalized by the psychological effects of gratitude. Gratitude, like other healing emotions, helps to secrete soothing metabolic juices that help us break down the food that we eat into glucose and energy particles.

Abraham caused God's name to be mentioned by all the travelers whom he entertained. For after they had eaten and drunk, and when they arose to bless Abraham, he said to them, "Is it of mine that you have eaten? Surely it is of what belongs to God that you have eaten. So praise and bless Him by whose word the world was created."

—*Judaism. Talmud*

Be not like those who honor their Gods in prosperity and curse them in adversity. In pleasure or pain, give thanks.

—*Judaism. Mekilta to Exodus 20:2*

One upon whom we bestow our kindness,
But will not express gratitude,
Is worse than a robber
Who carries away our belongings.

—*Yoruba Proverb*

Even if you cry your heart out, hurt your eyes by constant weeping, and even if you lead the life of an ascetic till the end of the world, all these untiring efforts of yours will not be able to make compensation for a tithe of His goodwill and kindness, for His bounties and munificence and for His mercy and charity in directing you towards the path of truth and religion.

—*Nahjul Balagha, Khutba 57*

The unworthy man is ungrateful, forgetful of benefits [done to him]. This ingratitude, this forgetfulness is congenial to mean people...But the worthy person is grateful and mindful of benefits done to him. This gratitude, this mindfulness, is congenial to the best people.

—*Buddhism*

The Four Debts of Gratitude, according to the Buddhist philosophy are:

1. The debt of gratitude to all living things including one's teachers
2. The debt of gratitude to one's father and mother
3. The debt of gratitude to one's ruler (king, emperor, etc.)
4. The debt of gratitude to Lord Buddha Himself, who alone can, by His grace, uplift one from the "doldrum of suffering" and bestow upon him the priceless peace and tranquility of Nirvana.

How to Cultivate a Grateful Mind

If doubts arise in the conscious mind, just say, "I am grateful for this lesson." Harmony between the conscious mind and the subconscious mind is very essential for successful attainment of any goal in human life. A house divided against itself cannot stand. A mind divided against itself cannot function!

The Law of Psychic Phenomena, by Dr. Thomson Hudson, opened my eyes to a new world of possibilities, and it opened a window to the Universe of the Mind. I studied the lectures on Mental Science by Judge Troward, a pioneer in this little-known field. The logical explanation of Judge Troward, his deep insights into the subject, and his dedication to research made me an ardent student and practitioner. My own understanding of Mental Science can be summarized into one sentence:

> "You can do anything you want to do, and you can be anybody you want to be, if you put your mind to it."

Most of us only use a fraction of our mind power, and need training in using this mysterious and marvelous apparatus. Before attempting to cultivate a grateful mind, you should have a good idea and solid training about the working of your own mind. According to Mental Science Principles, your world is a thought world. All the thoughts that you think constantly, whether thoughts of joy or sorrow, are translated into your everyday experience. From this it follows that to change your world, you have to simply change your thoughts.

For understanding purposes, we divide your mind into two categories, based on its distinct functions: the conscious mind and the subconscious mind:

> Your conscious mind gathers information using the five sense organs, and processes and compares with the help of the brain. Whatever thoughts you think again and again will become habitual and will sink into your subconscious mind, which will act on them as though it is a command received from the conscious mind—the master.

> Your subconscious mind is an obedient servant of the conscious mind. It does not argue or reason, as power of discrimination is not its faculty. Like a faithful and loyal servant, it will act on the command received from the master—the conscious mind. The subconscious mind is the storehouse of emotions and it is the very creative agent that weaves the tapestry of human emotions, feelings and experience. Thus if you think good, always using good thoughts as the raw material, the subconscious will weave good experience. Conversely, if you choose to cultivate bad thoughts, the subconscious mind will act on that command and weave the fabric of fear, sorrow and frustration. This is the only way the subconscious mind works.

Conscious mind is the mind that chooses. It is the master giving the command to your subconscious mind to build a hall of harmony or the shadow of sorrow and frustration depending upon the nature of thoughts you feed your mind constantly—hence the Biblical expression, "Whatever I have feared has fallen upon me."

The one cardinal principle of Mental Science to bear in mind at all times is that every thought you harbor in the secret chamber of your mind is a reminder to the subconscious mind to act on those thoughts and bring them as experience, events and conditions. The subconscious mind is not the rational mind; it is the order taking and order executing servant of the master—the conscious mind which alone is the rational, logical and reasoning mind. This one truth alone can save you a lot of sorrow and frustration and make you the architect of your destiny and the master of your fate. This is also the secret behind "the rich getting richer and the poor getting poorer." You become what you think all day long.

A healthy body thus becomes the direct result of a clean mind where harmonious thoughts dwell and reign. Peace of mind and health are not accidents nor are reserved for a privileged few—this is the constant result of harmonious thoughts and feelings. Based on the operation of the "Law of Being," whatever you believe will be translated into your life as experience, events and conditions by the power of the subconscious mind. The power of the subconscious mind is not to be taken lightly. It can gather information on an extra-sensorial basis; it transcends time and space, and is an inlet into the universal, all-knowing mind.

Hypnotic State

A hypnotic state is an induced state of awareness for the subconscious mind. It is a psychotherapeutic technique where the therapist prepares the subject's mind to receive any given suggestion as true. Because the subconscious mind does not argue, and the reasoning mind is kept in a state of abeyance, the subconscious mind acts upon whatever suggestions the therapist gives, acting on them as if they are true.

A distinct quality of the subconscious mind is that it is amenable to suggestions. The suggestion does not have to be from another person, as it can be self-induced auto-suggestion. Auto-suggestion is a valuable and effective tool in cultivating a grateful mind.

Positive Affirmation

Positive affirmations are nothing but auto suggestions given to the subconscious mind to transform itself to a grateful mind. A grateful mind is a creative mind. It is a tranquil mind, at peace with itself and the world. It is a content and calm mind, devoid of frustrations, restlessness and discontentment. Those affirmations are powerful suggestions given to the subconscious mind at a time where the conscious mind is in a state of obedience. The reasoning mind can either accept or reject suggestions, but if it is not alert, the suggestion will sink directly into the unquestioning subconscious mind. The most appropriate times for this suggestive therapy is dawn and dusk, or just before dozing off to sleep. These times are appropriate, because the subconscious mind is at a peak alert stage to receive the suggestions without any interference from the objective mind. It is the power of the conscious mind that prevents any suggestions from being delivered directly to the subconscious mind. It acts as the watchman at a gate, so that no intruding thoughts will enter the realm of the deeper layers without its approval.

For example, a friend of yours wants to trick you into believing that you are a dumb person. As soon as he called you "stupid," your conscious mind drew from its memory arguments against that statement. It recalls your SAT score which was above 1300, and you pulled an A- average in college; it reminds you as well that you have professional qualifications. Based on all these recalled memories, your conscious mind rejects his suggestions by laughing at it. But if the suggestion of you being "stupid" occurs during the waking hour, or just before falling asleep, the results could be totally different, as the power of the dominant mind is not alert to argue against the statement of your friend.

"What I have feared has fallen upon me" is a renowned Biblical statement which is based on the law of subconscious. Any fears that we dwell on continuously become a suggestion that the subconscious accepts as true; thus it will act on it, and eventually become a manifested reality. Therefore, it is necessary to be vigilant to cast negative thoughts out of our consciousness, designating them as worthless. Fear of failure, for example, has held many a young man and woman from becoming successful in their chosen field of endeavor.

The most important thing to remember at all times is the interaction between the conscious mind and the subconscious minds. As soon as the fear thought arises, replace it with a "faith thought." Faith is a real antidote for fear. Let the thought arise, but don't dwell on it. Instead, repeat three times, "I am grateful for this experience."

Gratitude Dispels Fears

"I am grateful for this experience" is an effective mantra to recite at all times. It helps to not only negate emotions such as fear, but stimulates a positive emotion of gratitude, which opens the floodgate of grace for you to find a solution to the problem at hand. A grateful attitude places you in a positive state of ease, helping you to tackle any problem that you face. It also helps you to avoid a rash reaction, which most of us feel compelled to fall for. A grateful mind is a creative and calm mind that is ready to tackle the situation at hand. It can find a solution to the problem more easily than an agitated mind engulfed in fears. A reacting mind is at the mercy of the outside world; it is always controlled by outside forces. When you act, you are a master, but when you react, you are a slave, vulnerable to the actions of others. You become a doormat for others to step on at their will. Thus any person who is willing to practice gratitude will be saved from the wrath of a weak and weary reacting mind.

Resist Not Him That Is Evil

In Matthew 5:38 and 39, Jesus said, "You have heard that it was said, an eye for an eye and a tooth for a tooth; but I say unto you, resist not him that is evil."

Evil in a metaphysical sense is a condition caused by the absence of divinity (which is absolute goodness). When a person tries to resist evil, he is resorting to judgment and dwelling on the evil. According to the Law of Mental Science, you become that you think all day long. Thus the person who is determined to resist evil might become evil himself, which defeats the very purpose of removing the evil from the consciousness. To cement this power of not resisting the evil, the great master added another device: be indifferent to evil. You cannot condone evil, as it amounts to participating. Neither do you condemn evil, which amounts to judgment. Just like darkness can only be dispelled by light, so is evil which can be transformed into goodness by introducing divinity to the situation.

The power of gratitude can help anyone practice the Lord's advice to "resist not him that is evil." In the practice of grati-tude, the emphasis is on the present. Even when a not-so-good experience occurs, we can recite our manta, "I am grateful for this experience." A positive welcome to the negative experience in fact neutralizes the negative, and the power of gratitude over-comes the effects of negative like the introduction of a candle lit in a room immersed in darkness. It not only dispels darkness— it brightens up the room with the light. Overwhelmed by the power of gratitude, the negative situation transforms itself into a positive one. Gratitude is always the way to win over any of the negative experiences that we face.

The following positive affirmations will help you cultivate a grateful attitude:

I am grateful for my happy life.

I am grateful for my loving father and mother.

I am grateful for my good health.

I am grateful for my loving wife/husband.

I am grateful for my loving children.

I am grateful for my job/profession.

I am grateful for my dog/cat.

I am grateful for my employer.

I am grateful for my good friends.

I am grateful for my good life in the USA.

I am grateful for my good education.

I am grateful for my Karma.

I am grateful for this experience.

I am grateful for this house.

I am grateful for my car.

I am grateful for my food.

I am grateful for my grades.

I am grateful for the help of my teachers.

I am grateful for the books I read and the authors who wrote them.

I am grateful that I can read.

I am grateful that I can see.

I am grateful that I can hear.

I am grateful that I can smell.

I am grateful that I can feel.

I am grateful for this day.

CHAPTER THREE

The Great Transformer

As the alarm clock rings at 6:00 on a Monday morning, leap out of bed to start another work week filled with excitement and the anticipation of joyous accomplishments and corporate challenges. But before getting out of the bed, say a prayer of gratitude as follows:

> Oh, Creator of all things
> Kindly accept my gratitude for another day
> Many people who went to sleep last night
> Did not wake up, yet you gave me this day
> To shine, dazzle, and do my duty.

You can customize this gratitude prayer any way you want according to your religious faith, spiritual insights, and metaphysical incantations. A day begun with gratitude, filled with gratitude, and ending with gratitude will undoubtedly be a day of joyous achievements at the personal and business levels. As Jesus Himself said, "Seek ye first the kingdom of God and its righteousness, and everything shall be added unto you." By showing our gratitude to our creator (according to one's belief), you will open the very channel to the reservoir of infinite wisdom; this will promote not only peace and tranquility for ourselves, but for others around us as well.

Your business life is nothing but an extension of your personal life, and the thoughts that fill your mind most of the time dictate the quality of your character. For example, if you are considerate of your family members at home, you will definitely show that quality when you are with your associates at work. If you cultivate thoughts of gratitude, it will lead to gratitude as a way of life, which will be more fulfilling and rewarding.

After your morning rituals and prayer of gratitude, leave home in a cordial and peaceful way. Take leave of your wife or husband and children, expressing your love and gratitude for their love and support. Never indulge in an argument with your spouse or other family members before leaving home. Even if it happens, stay back a few minutes to cool your mind before saying goodbye.

It is equally important to keep your mind in balance while on the road. You can listen to some inspiring messages or light music that will uplift your mind. If there is more traffic than usual, do not get upset. Instead, feel good about all the drivers on the road, and give thanks for a smooth flow of traffic. When you expect the best, you get the best. A grateful mind is a creative mind, willing and able to create harmonious circumstances (even harmonious traffic flow). A sense of gratitude is a spiritual compass that will quiet your mind on your journey through the trials and tribulations of everyday life, including a crowded expressway.

"Love To-Do" List

Almost all members of the corporate workforce, starting from the secretary to the president or CEO, maintain a "to-do list." From today onwards, change the name of that list to "love to-do." The moment you call it a "love to-do" list, a chemical change takes place in your mind. Many corporate inhabitants hate what they do; because they hate what they do, they do not advance in their career, and the quality of work becomes of mediocre caliber. With gratitude in every undertaking, you will begin to love what you do. There are many people who are laid off or cannot find a job—yet you are blessed with a job. Express your gratitude every day before starting the job, and you will discover that your job has become joyous and challenging.

Fake It 'Til You Make It

There is a deep-rooted Mental Science Principle involved in the above simple statement. Even if your job is boring and routine, bring some enthusiasm and life to the job. Say it several times: "I love this job," and keep doing it. When you say, "I love my job," there is a silent dialogue taking place in the inner chambers of your mind. Your subconscious mind, that little internal powerhouse within you, says as follows: "My master (the conscious mind) thinks that he/she loves his/her job. Let me make sure that he/she truly enjoys it."

The subconscious mind does not know the difference between synthetic (fake) experience and an actual experience. It does not argue. It accepts whatever the mastermind (conscious mind) commands it to do, and will bring that command to its intended conclusion. The great Harvard psychologist William James advocated his famous "act as if" principle. Act as if you are happy, and you will be happy. Act as if you are successful, you will be successful. Hence the saying "Fake it 'til you make it."

Thus creating a "love to-do" list literally shifts your state of mind, and at the end of the day, you will have not only completed work of the tasks you set out to do—you will have done it with love. Love what you hate, and bless that hates you. When you follow this principle of harmony, you will run out of things to hate, and any hatred that comes towards you will be transformed to blessings. Spiritually speaking, to bless means to release one's unconditional love towards the other. When you master the principles of gratitude, you will still have to solve problems at work and at home, but your own modus operandi has undergone a radical change for the better.

Finish Line

From today onwards, do not use the word "deadline," which has negative psychological connotations, which are not even worthy of dwelling on further. Just call it a "finish line," which shows that you have finished the assignment by the finish line date. Every time you think of a finish line date for a project, imagine before your mind's eye running the prestigious derby. The imagination invokes the famous racehorse of pride, prestige and accomplishment. It helps to remove the negative feelings of dread and fear (if you cannot meet the deadline) and the ensuing stress associated with such negativity. Before you accept the new assignment, express your gratitude for the assignment, and feel good about it. When you feel good, you will do good. An expression of gratitude will remove the dirt of negativity and fear from your mind, and will create fertile, receptive conditions for the new assignment.

Make the finish line your own. You may have received it from your boss, but when you make it your own, there is a personal commitment to the project. With a sense of gratitude, all of your creative channels will be open to help you complete the assignment on time. At every step of the way, keep an open mind, and allow yourself to be guided. The great inventor and genius Thomas Edison said, "Ideas are in the air." All that we need is a highly receptive mind.

An "Ungrateful Boss"

Many times, a corporate executive makes a comment like this: "Gopi, you do not know my boss. He is ungrateful and inconsiderate." The real problem is not the boss, but the executive who has a negative attitude towards the boss. When you work for a large corporation, you are not working for any person. A corporation is an artificial person created by law and represented by all the employees, including the CEO representing it. Rather than focusing on the limitations of the boss, focus on the positive. Write down the good qualities of the boss and saturate your mind with those personality traits. When you get an opportunity, sincerely praise those qualities in him or her. Most of the time, your opinions are influenced by the biases and prejudices of your own mind. The above exercise will eliminate those biased opinions from the surface and deeper layers of the mind. Again, "Love what you hate, and bless what hates you."

Gratitude Eliminates Stress

Stress is the body's response to negative thoughts, embedded in fear. Living in fear causes chronic stress and serious harmful health effects. When chronically stressed, the brain secretes a hormone called ACTH. This hormone influences the adrenal gland to secrete cortisol. While cortisol acts as a repair hormone in the short run, its continuous secretion is very harmful by not only obstructing the flow of the immune cells, but by weakening the strength of the already-existing immune cells in the body. Thus chronic stress can cause the breakdown of our immune system, inviting infections and other disorders to our otherwise healthy body.

A grateful attitude reduces stress, and, if practiced daily, can even eliminate dangerous stress levels altogether, thus removing the need for deadly chemicals to be secreted by the brain. Even when you have lousy schedules and "finish lines" to reach, an ounce of gratitude will remove a ton of stress from your mental sphere. When positive attitudes permeate the deeper layers of the mind, the result is healing emotions that can transform you to be a wholesome, grateful individual. As your body exists only in your mind, a mind filled with peaceful gratitude alone promote a healthy and harmonious body devoid of any uneasiness which we call disease (dis+ease = disease—not at ease).

Gratitude is an elixir for a healthy mind and healthy body. It assures contentment. If you dwell on what you have, and be thankful for the blessings, it helps you to count your blessings on a daily basis. A mind filled with gratitude alone is ready to receive more blessings whether it be perfect health, happiness, wealth, career change or enhancement.

A Journal Of Gratitude (JOG)

Knowledge is utterly useless unless you can apply it to improve the quality of everyday life. The best way to practice gratitude is to keep a journal of gratitude. Every day, spend a few minutes to write down the experiences, events and people to whom you are grateful. In addition, before going to sleep, feel your gratitude for those events, experiences, and fellow human beings. End this spiritual ritual by expressing your gratitude to the creator for one more joyous day on Earth. Gratitude opens the channels of healing—healing for the body and the mind, from a source unknown to us the mortals. When Ralph Waldo Emerson said, "All I have seen teaches me to trust the creator for all I have not seen," he was, in a way, expressing his own gratitude for all the inner wisdom he enjoyed.

Journal Of Gratitude

Number	Name of Person, Event, Experience	Lesson Learned
1	My pet died this morning. Thank you for all the good times you spend with me and my family. I express my sincere gratitude for	Life is fleeting. It is here now but may not be here the next moment.

your loving company and pleasing acrobats.

2	I am about to get into the car to go to work and I noticed a flat tire.	I am grateful for this experience. What more can I ask? I got a flat tire on my driveway.
3	My wife called me a jerk.	I kept quiet. She thinks I am useless (jerk). Maybe in this instance I sat on the couch watching TV, without helping her with daily chores. Mentally, I recite, "I am sorry, dear."
4	Received a "thank you" card from a church.	Immediately send a "gratus card" as a gesture of appreciation. *A copy of the Gratus card is in the appendix*

Love To Do List

1	10:00 AM	Meeting with the boss about our new marketing program.
2	11:30 AM	Meeting with Secretary about finishing the budget review for the first quarter.
3	12:00 PM–1:00 PM	Lunch with the new client to discuss the order execution finish line.

4	1:00 PM	Review of today's mail (including e-mails with the secretary/assistant).
5	2:00 PM	Return telephone calls for the day.
6	3:00 PM	Meeting with the marketing manager about the new marketing initiatives for the new product.
7	4:00 PM	Meeting with the secretary to finish the pending correspondence.

Healing Power of Gratitude

Gratitude is the mother of all healing emotions, and as such, it induces the physical body to promote its immune system, which in turn protects the body against all illness caused by bacteria, microbes, parasites and other foreign substances. Gratitude also promotes other healing emotions like unconditional love, forgiveness, compassion, mercy and charity. As you focus on life's challenges with gratitude, the dark shadows of negativity will begin to dissipate from life. A grateful heart is an invitation to more blessings to come into your life. Gratitude is recognition of things as they are. It simply acknowledges the divine order of purpose. It does not criticize events as they unfold; it simply accepts them with gratitude.

Thought and Emotion

Every intense thought or emotional thought produces its corresponding emotions. If it is a hurting thought, it will produce hurting emotions, and if it is a healing thought, it will express healing emotions. Every emotion is a physical response of the body to an intense or chronic thought. The challenge of every human being is to understand the relationship between thought and emotion, and to practice strong healing thoughts which, when repeated, produce healing emotions in the individual.

Every individual has the ability to produce healing emotions at will, having thus understood the universal principle that everything multiplies after its kind. The human mind, when understood properly, is an instrument of perception, capable of being trained and transformed to promote healing and harmony within the individual. Gratitude is one major healing emotion, and when cultivated as a habit, it can impact the individual in a very positive way. When you understand the healing power of gratitude, and practice it in every aspect of life, it becomes a way of life, and a path to peace and prosperity.

Healing the Mind, Healing the Body

You cannot heal the body without healing the mind first, because your body exists only in your mind. This healed mind, which is the playground of healing thought, will promote a healthy and harmonious body. Perfect health is not an accident; it is the result of cultivating healing thoughts and corresponding healing emotions. Healing is every man's birthright, he has the power to invoke that healer within once he understands and respects the working of the human mind. It is within the reach of everyone to heal the mind and heal the body, and with simple practice of everyday gratitude, the task is made even simpler for everyone who attempts to be healed.

The history of healing in ancient times is mired in mystery, and very often colored with a tint of superstition. The priests and holy men of old were said to possess the supernatural power of healing the sick and weary mortals. The power to heal was believed to be the power directly granted by God to such holy people. The method and procedures used to heal were of different natures in different parts of the world.

Lord Jesus Himself exercised this power to heal the sick, as recorded in Matthew 9:28-30 (King James Version): And when he was come into the house the blind men came to him, and Jesus said to them, believe ye that I am able to do this? They said unto him, yea Lord. Then he touched their eyes, saying, according to your faith be it unto you. And their eyes were opened, and Jesus strictly charged them, saying, see that no man know it.

The key in this whole account of healing is the Lord affirming their faith in Him to heal. The blind men believed that Jesus could give them their sight back. Their faith, their conviction and their grateful mental attitude enabled them to receive their eyesight. And Jesus also warned them that the should "see that no man know it." He wanted to make sure that their faith was sealed once and for all, lest by talking to people who could punch holes in their faith, the formerly blind man could lose his sight again.

Hidden here is an important mental science principle: According to your faith be it unto you. The Law of Faith is the Law of Belief. It is a function of the subconscious mind that is the basis of our mind power, which controls and regulates all the vital functions of the body. Without the full cooperation of the subconscious mind, healing is impossible. Subconscious mind is the healer. It is capable of bringing healing to any man who believes in it. All the rituals and procedures practiced in healing at different parts of the world is only intended to induce the subconscious mind to the idea of healing.

Gratitude Tames the Subconscious Mind

Gratitude has the ability to ease the task of taming the subconscious mind. Faith is an essential element to the subconscious mind, and without faith no one can invoke the healing power of the subconscious mind. Doubt is the only known enemy of faith. Doubts create fear; fear is an epitome of negativity which flushes out every ounce of faith from the mind. A faithless mind can be compared to only a lifeless body. It is the faith that emboldens the mind; it fuels the mental machine to tackle the task presented to it, no matter what it is. Thus the challenge to any human being in following faith in one's mind is elimination of doubt from the conscious mind. This task is easily handled by the power of gratitude.

Gratitude Eliminates Negativity

Gratitude has the ability to erase negativity from the sphere of the mind. Without the fuel of negativity, no fear can spring up in the mind, and thus the power of gratitude retains the faith without erosion. A mind devoid of fear is the mind amenable to suggestion, like fertile soil in which the seeds of any kind germinate and sprout with the explosive energy of enthusiasm. In such a mind anchored in faith, the power of the subconscious to heal can be induced easily and effectively with minimum effort.

The importance of gratitude in healing the mind and healing the body cannot be over-emphasized. Gratitude, in essence, is the spiritual straw with which we can all draw the divine grace into our daily life. An ounce of gratitude can eliminate a ton of negativity from the mind, just like a small lighted candle can erase total darkness from any dark room into which it is introduced.

Psychoneuroimmunology /
The Science of Healing Emotions

Psychoneuroimmunology is a new branch of medical science that studies the effects of thoughts and emotions on the body's immune system. It seeks to establish a link between our thoughts and their effects on the body's ability to enhance or weaken the function of the immune cells. With advanced research at various centers of higher learning, such as Harvard and NIS, scientists have already established a link between body and mind. The wellbeing and welfare of the physical body, as the ancient psychologists and metaphysicians already knew, depended mainly on the types of thoughts one entertained in the secret chamber of one's own mind. A clear mind, as now the science has proven, can indeed help promote vibrant health in the individual.

The famous Harvard study in the field of mind/body connection, pioneered in the seventies, discovered the presence of receptors on our immune cells. The result of this study confirmed the effect of various emotions on the body's immune system. The results of this research study prove only one thing: we hold in our head (or heart) the key to our immune system—gratitude (a grateful attitude). A survey of the study is given below, as it definitely sheds light on the link between emotions and their philosophical response.

Psychoneuroimmunology

A Harvard study in the seventies discovered receptors on our immune cells for neuropeptides. Neuropeptides are chemicals produced by the brain that vary with our emotions. The results of this study point to the simple fact that your immune system is listening to your mental talk. How you think is how you feel. When someone tells you that you're only as old as you feel, believe it.

Below are the results of a study conducted on students, separated into two sections, negative and positive states.

Negative States

Bereavement	Decreased lymphocyte proliferation.
Pessimistic States	Decreased lymphocyte reactivity; decreased T-cell effectiveness.
Academic Stress	Decreased NK (natural killer) cell activity; decreased T-cells; decrease in certain immune chemicals; increased susceptibility to herpes virus; decreased immunoglobulin A;

	increased blood levels of Epstein-Barr virus.
Depression	Decreased T-cells; decreased number and function of lymphocytes; decreased NK cells.
Loneliness	Decreased NK cells activity.
Chronic Stress	Decreased T-cells; decreased NK cells; decreased B-cells; increased blood levels of Epstein-Barr virus.
Divorce/Separation/ Poor Marital Quality	Decreased lymphocyte function; increased blood levels of Epstein-Barr virus; decreased T-cell effectiveness.
Expressed need for power and control	Decreased NK activity; decreased lymphocytes.
Negative behavior during discussions of marital problems	Decreased NK activity; decreased macrophages; increased blood levels of Epstein-Barr virus; increase in certain T-cells; decreased immunity by mitogen tests.

Positive States

Satisfying personal relationships and social support	Increased lymphocyte function; increased NK activity; increased immunity by mitogen tests; increased immune response to hepatitis B vaccine.

Healing Chemicals

The human brain is the most wonderful chemical factory in the world. The most modern pharmaceutical companies are learning to imitate this nature's mystical chemical factory. Every cell in the body, scientists now conclude, is in communication with the brain. Every change in our mood or emotion is translated at the cellular level with the help of the nerve proteins called neuropeptides. Though neuropeptides are produced mainly in the brain, they are also produced by other organs like the stomach. Basically, neuropeptides carry the message of healing and a feeling of wellness. The research by famous scientist Dr. Pert in this field of neuropeptides is remarkable. They are called ligands (which come from the Latin word *ligane* which means to build). All neuropeptides bind to the receptors in the cell to affect the change at the cellular level. For an intense journey into the world of neuropeptides, the reader is directed to read the book *Molecules of Emotion* by Dr. Pert.

Scientists are discovering in research labs what philosophers and metaphysicians have discovered in minute details hundreds of years ago, based on scriptural texts that were written over thousands of years ago in different parts of the world. Man indeed has the power to choose his own destiny by changing the pattern of thoughts he entertained in the secret chamber of his own mind. Healing, or a healed state of body and mind, is the birthright of every human being, and it is well within reach of every man and woman regardless of his/her color, race, religion or gender.

Disease As A Blessing

The first and foremost step to invoke healing is accepting the disease with gratitude as a blessing. Many times, the patient's own denial of the onset of disease acts as a resistance to the healing to take place. But the feeling of gratitude and welcoming the disease with gratitude makes it easy to remove the resistance of denial from the patient's own mind. A grateful mind is like a pure piece of white cloth with no stains of negativity. A mind devoid of any negativity is a mind ready to receive healing.

The thirteenth century mystical poet Rumi said it eloquently in his "Grief as a Blessing."

> I saw grief drinking a cup of sorrow and called out, "It tastes sweet, does it not?"
> "You have caught me," grief answered, "And you have ruined my business; how can I sell Sorrow when you know it is a blessing?"

Every blessing is a spiritual stepping stone that takes us closer and closer to the spiritual realization that indeed we are the authors of our own joy and sorrow. Events such as the death of a dear one plunge us into sorrow, mainly because of our feelings of personal loss, guilt for an act of commission, or perhaps guilt for an act of omission towards the departed. For young ones and many adults as well, it is due to the ignorance of the Law of Life, which includes a point known as death. Any organism that is born has to die, generally after completing its life cycle, and many times before the end of the life cycle. The organism has taken a toll of wear and tear, due to lifestyle. Every sorrow comes to teach us a lesson; learn the lesson and move on to complete your mission in life. Always keep an open mind to accept every event in life with gratitude, which essentially is a spiritual acknowledgement that all is well. The world is on purpose, you are on purpose, and there are no accidents in the universe.

Being with the Mind

Every healing process begins with healing the mind. You can begin the healing process with a gratitude for the afflictions. Gratitude, as the mother of all healing emotions, can help purify the mind by cleansing and flushing out negative hurting emotions like fear, hatred, greed, jealousy, and judgment. That alone is the foundation for any healing process.

The time-tested peace prayer of St. Francis of Assisi, the famous Christian monk who lived and prayed in the thirteenth century, is in fact a healing prayer for everyone afflicted or otherwise. His famous prayer reads:

Lord make me an instrument of your peace—
Where there is hatred, let me sow love;
Where there is injury, pardon; where there is doubt, faith;
Where there is despair, hope;
Where there is darkness, light;
And where there is sadness, joy.
Oh Divine Master that I may not so much seek,
To be consoled as to console,
To be understood as to understand,
To be loved as to love,
For it is in giving that we receive,
It is in pardoning that we are pardoned,
And it is in dying that we are born to eternal life.

Translating this holy monk's prayer into the realm of healing, one must aspire to heal others before being healed from any affliction affecting the mind or the body. The root of the word *heal* can be traced back to its original word, which meant *whole* or *hearty*. Basically, we are created whole, but because of our thought, speech and living patterns of emotional living, we have forgotten our natural state of healing and harmony. This healing does not only mean healing the afflicted body, but discovering our true nature, which is nothing less than bliss and pure harmony. Every thought, speech and deed we perform should be directed towards the discovery of the true self, which is developed in healing and bliss.

Cause and Effect

Understanding the Law of Cause and Effect will help us alleviate most of our suffering. The Law of Karma, which is based on cause and effect, states that everyone has to reap the consequences of his karma (actions) as the law itself is very impersonal. For example, a child unaware of the Law of Karma puts her hand in the fire , they will be burnt, as the function of the heat is to burn—though the child was innocent and too young to understand it.

Every karma or action begins with a thought in one's mind. A thought when focused on continuously becomes a burning desire. Any deep-rooted desire will attract all elements necessary to translate that desire into its natural conclusion—its fulfillment in the domain of matter.

Every desire begins with a thought—the basic building block of spirit. Respectful thoughts weave themselves into a panoramic visualization until its material equivalent is created. Once we experience the outcome, we cannot complain that we did not wish to have it. So it is very essential to check every thought that we create and sustain in the realm of our conscious mind.

The cause of every experience we have in our life, whether a physical affliction or mental agony, arises out of strong and sustained thoughts. Having understood the Law of Cause and Effect and the working of our own mind, we will tend to be more careful in entertaining negative thoughts as they evolve themselves into experiences of agony frustration, and pain.

An Alcoholic and a Priest

The comparison of an alcoholic and a priest is made only to shed light on working of the thoughts in transforming two individuals to their present state of mind. The alcoholic was not an addict when he started to drink. He was a social elite having a drink or two at social occasions. But the pressures of everyday life at work or at home tempted him to resort to alcohol as a way of forgetting his everyday problems, which brought him to his present-day status as an addict. He did not become an addict overnight; it was a gradual process of drinking for years. Though it started with a single peg of alcohol, the repeated act of drinking made him the slave of a cruel habit. If he had diverted his thoughts to something more creative in order to solve the problems of life's pressures, he would have remained a social drinker with only one or two drinks occasionally at social gatherings.

The priest, on the other hand, was a theology student, and his repeated thoughts about theology and his career made him complete school and become a priest. His sustained thoughts of becoming a priest, and his ability to serve the Lord propelled him to study and finish the coursework, though at times it was hard on him to get up in the morning and go to school.

The story of the alcoholic and the priest reveals the power of thoughts to transform people. But the sad part in the story is that the alcoholic probably was not aware of the power of thought, as many alcoholics think they can quit at any time. The wise man knows that habit is a merciless master, and he can deliberately choose to cultivate healing habits like gratitude, compassion, love and forgiveness. Thought by thought, word by word, and deed by deed, we can transform ourselves from an unlettered to lettered, rich to poor, or sick to healthy individual. The secret is to know the Law of Cause and Effect.

- Nothing happens without a cause.
- Focus on the cause and not the effect to bring any change.
- After changing the cause, patiently wait for the transformation.

In the phenomenal world of matter, man's ability to convert spirit (unmanifested) into any form of matter (the manifested) depends on his understanding of thought power and the relation between the conscious mind and the subconscious mind. The ability to think and imagine is God-like; using thought power, man creates his own world. Thus thoughts are the causes—conditions are simply effects. Only by directing the flow of thoughts can man change his destiny and change his conditions. Most of the time, however, without understanding the Law of Cause and Effect, we waste our time and efforts to change the conditions, and get even more frustrated as nothing changes. One must always remember that by changing causes, one can change conditions, which are nothing but the visible offsprings of one or more causes.

Example of a Matchstick

The great teaching of Jainism compares a negative thought or attitude to a burning matchstick. A burning matchstick destroys itself before it can burn, down to ashes, everything in its path. Every negative thought we entertain in our mind hurts us before it could hurt anybody else. Understanding this profound truth alone is worthwhile, and the practice of it can eliminate much of our suffering. Any negative thought is more harmful than any bacteria or germ that forms inside our physical body. Many times, those harmful bacteria and parasites are held in check by our own strong immune system. But when it comes to our mind, we are not aware of the damage it could cause to our mind and body.

Here we can use our power of discrimination and consciously employ gratitude, not only as a spiritual cleanser, but also as a very powerful healing agent. Since gratitude removes negativity from the conscious mind, the thought is disarmed and rendered powerless, and loses its power to harm or hurt. Since we constantly express gratitude for every event that happens in our life, whether it produces pain or pleasure, the mind is constantly cleansed and healed. Such a clean mind alone can produce healing thoughts to sustain a healthy and harmonious body.

Wish for Others What You Wish for Yourself

Another famous teaching of Jainism reaffirms the importance of practicing the golden rule, "Treat others the way you like to be treated." The philosophy of Jainism teaches us to wish for others what we wish for ourselves. For example, if you wish good health, harmony and wealth for yourself, you must also wish for others the same good health, harmony and wealth. It brings out a fundamental spiritual principle that even if one person remains unhappy in the world, you will not be able to sustain happiness for a long time.

Unity of Spirit

There is only one Universe that is united in the power of spirit. All life on earth is connected by this indescribable power of spirit. The very understanding that the life pulsating in us is the spark of the same spirit that is throbbing as life in another living being; even in a blade of grass that sways with the breeze is going to help us understand the unity of spirit. There is a master computer called *universal consciousness* or *universal mind*, to which we are all connected. As the great philosopher Ralph Emerson put it, when we realize this spiritual connection we become...

> Owner of the spirit,
> Of the seven stars and the solar year,
> Of Caesar's hand and Plato's brain,
> Of the Lord Jesus' heart and Shakespeare's strain.

As we remove the different layers of our mask of self-deception, and the unity of spirit becomes clear, our first act of freedom will be to recognize our spiritual brothers and sisters who are spread across the length and breadth of our ancestral home, which we lovingly call this world. It is with this spiritual intention in mind that the Lord Jesus Christ prayed; this later came to be known as the Lord's Prayer:

> Our Father, who art in heaven,
> Hallowed be thy name,

Thy kingdom come on earth,
As it is in heaven,
Give us this day our daily bread,
Forgive our debts as we forgive our debtors,
Lead us not into temptation but deliver us from evil,
For thine is the kingdom, power and the glory forever...
    amen.

The Lord's Prayer in every essence is a prayer of gratitude that can be proclaimed to evoke healing in everyday life. Praising the Holy Name is a spiritual expression of gratitude that induces the flow of healing energy. *Thy kingdom* is a referral to the "domain of spirit," and prayer is to move the same spirit in ourselves. This prayer also acknowledges that we are all renters as we lease the domain of spirit for a temporary life cycle as, "Thine is the kingdom, power and glory forever."

We Are All Temps

Years ago, I called a friend who worked in a big corporate office. The receptionist, whose name was Jennifer, answered the phone and told me that my friend was out of the office. I asked Jennifer, "Do you know when he is supposed to be back in the office?" She answered, "Sir, I have no idea, because I am just a temp here." There was a sad tonality in her voice. To perk her up, I told her, "Jennifer, in reality, we are all temps here." She got a kick out of it and had a good laugh.

After I finished the telephone conversation, I began to ponder the profound nature of the simple statement that I'd uttered at the spur of the moment. I remember this statement at all times to remain aware of the transient nature of life on earth.

A regular reminder that "we are all temps here" gives us a different perceptive, especially when emotions run high and arguments flare up. Life is as impermanent as a dewdrop rolling on one's palm; a prayer of gratitude every day as we open our eyes will get us off to a good start—and surely a harmonious one. As the great Mahatma Gandhi said, "There is no way to gratitude, gratitude is the way." A grateful attitude in all our dealings with the outside world, in our interpersonal relationships, and in our approach to any problem will definitely pave the way for harmonious solutions to all our daily ailments.

Gratitude—The Gateway

Gratitude is the gateway to spiritual living. Spiritual living only means living in tune with spirit. It does not mean abandoning the world, retreating to the forest, and leading the life of a recluse. It is happiness as it comes naturally. Spiritual living is the state of mind, where conflict is solved or resolved by staying in tune with the spirit. Spiritual living is natural living as our innate nature is spirit. The very source of existence is spirit, as the word *spirit* originates from the Latin word *spiritus*, meaning to "breathe."

The Three Questions

1. What is spirit?   Energy in its primordial form.

2. Where is spirit?   Everywhere.

3. How can I experience my spirit?   You are already doing it.

Being with Gratitude

The powerful healing emotions generated by gratitude open the door to limitless possibilities of spiritual living where peace and harmony alone reign. Simple acts of gratitude practiced on a daily basis awaken the spiritual power lying dormant in everyone. As the famous German mystic Mister Echart said,

"The only prayer you say in your life is a prayer of gratitude. It will suffice."

So begin every day as you wake up with a prayer of gratitude for another beautiful day. You can create your own prayer of gratitude based on your belief systems or religious background. It can also be a generic one as follows: "I am grateful for another beautiful day." Gratitude awakens the spirit in you. It is said that a piece of iron, when charged, can lift five times its weight, but when it is discharged, it loses its power to lift a feather. A grateful person appears to be inspired at all times and he is content with whatever comes on the way; he is convinced that there are no accidents in the universe. The world is on purpose; he is one purpose and life unfolds as it is. He is there to simply accept it with gratitude. Being inspired really means being in tune with spirit, surrounded by spirit, propelled by spirit, or enveloped in spirit. To those who understand this, spiritual living comes naturally, understanding that the state of harmony rests on the pillars of spirit as one walks through its corridors day and night.

New Channels, New Ways

The great Pathanjali Maharushi, a great proponent of yoga and the author of *Eight Limbs of Yoga*, lived more than a thousand years ago. He said, "When you are inspired...dormant forces, faculties, and talents become alive, and you discover yourself to be a greater person by far than you ever dreamed yourself to be."

An inspired person is a non-judgmental person, as he knows in his gut that being judgmental is a negative block on the path of self discovery. Because of his grateful living—living in gratitude—he simply observes the flow of events as witness, always nonjudgmental, and accepts the world as it is. He allows the higher power to operate on every aspect of life, as his judgmental interferences only slows down and in most cases blocks the opening of new channels and faculties. His conscious acceptance of divine order and purpose, that which gratitude is, allows the subconscious mind to align itself with the universal mind, so as to bring into manifestation whatever the desires are. In the process, his own faculties get awakened, and new ideas and purpose dawn on the horizon of his thought world, which make him a creative genius. This is what Pathanjali meant when he said, "When you are inspired, new channels open up, and new faculties get awakened."

Spiritual Biology

The term Spiritual Biology is a unique one in as much as it denotes the role of spirits in creating our physical body, which in fact is the sum total of our thoughts. A unique trait of every human is his ability to think, that is, to allocate a portion of his consciousness to anything he chooses. The basic building block of consciousness is spirit, and the basic building block of spirit is thought. To think is to form; form always implies time, and space goes with form. There can be no form without space, and no space without time. Thus, thought exists in the field of time and space.

Whenever you engage in the act of thinking, you are indeed 'forming' spiritual prototypes. Since individuals are free to think anything they want, they are free to form anything they choose. Therefore, it is clear that we can form limitations, and we do that very often. Similarly, we can form expansions and possibilities the same way, as the technique is the same. Simply said, we think and we form. Let us take the example of a potter. He has the clay as the raw material, and the potting wheel which simply rotates. He feeds the clay and the wheel to make different types of pottery. It could be a vessel to contain water, or a flower pot, or a tea cup. The clay is the same raw material; the potter simply supplies the imagination, and the pottery is made.

The same is true of a thinker—the thought maker. He can think of limitations with the same unmanifested spirit, or he can simply power the same spirit to make thoughts or expanding possibilities. The process is the same, the raw material is the same, but you simply provide the thought. Whatever you hold in your mind longer becomes your dominant thought. As the great Buddha said, "Whatever dominant thoughts you entertain in your mind, that alone you shall become."

As Pathanjali, the great proponent of yoga who is said to have lived in 400 B.C., said: *Yogas chittavrithi nirodha*. It means that union with God or the Higher Power happens when you cease mental activity. The same thing is echoed in Vedas, which proclaims, *AHAM BRAHMASMI*. Thus, when you think you are working with spirit, that primordial energy, into shapes—and when you stop differentiating the energy into this and that—the consciousness remains whole without any forms. Because there is no form (no longer), and there is no space which assumes time. Thus it is clear that "Kingdom of God is within." When the form and thought become one and the same, there is no external world, and you realize the truth that "I am He." Thus our thoughts create our world.

When thoughts cease, there is no world, and there are no formations. The manifested energy into the unmanifested and the spirit slip back into the primordial energy which the quantum physicist calls quantum soup.

The example given in Upanishads is that of a spider which creates its web out of itself and sits in the center of it. In the same way, you and I create our world with thoughts, and sit in the center of it. It simply means that you are the architect of your external world; the joy, the sorrow, the success, the failures, the wealth, the health and the connection or the disconnection you experience is the result of your very thinking. The key is to <u>focus</u> on that which you want to see manifested in your life.

Hence the Bible says, "What I have feared has fallen upon me." On a positive note, expect the best, and get the best.

In the beginning there was the Word; the Word was with God, and the Word was God (John 1:1). The word is simply the sound vibration of spirit—an expression of thought. Both philosophy and religion are in agreement that, in the beginning, there was nothing in the universe but unmanifested energy or spirit. The Egyptians called it *Ka,* the Hindus called it *prana*, and the Chinese called it *chi*—the same primordial spirit. The Supreme Law of Spirit is harmony, and the only mode of activity that can be attributed to spirit is thought. Since we cannot think without form, all that we see as the manifested is the formation of spirit. Thus energy formation of spirit is the exhibition of thought—the only mode of activity of spirit.

According to Hindu philosophy, it is Brahma, the creator which has become "created—the world." Thus, the primordial energy in its creative aspect has become everything that is ever created. Just like the seed containing a potential tree, the thought is the spiritual seed that contains the potential manifested world. Thus both the world of joy and the world of sorrow hide in the tiny yet powerful spiritual seed called thought.

Understanding this basic truth that you alone create your world, based on the nature of thought you entertain in your mind all day along, literally hands you the key to the secret of creation. The only creative power in the world is thought, that spiritual seed; though it is very tiny, it contains all the possibilities of your world. It is a great truth that was embodied by the great Master, "What you sow, that alone you shall reap." The same truth is echoed in the great Hindu Law of Karma: do not expect to reap apples if you sow the seeds of oranges.

Spiritual Biology is a term I have coined to impress upon humankind the need to understand our spiritual nature so that each one of us can choose to make for oneself a world of harmony, peace, good health and prosperity. At present, we are using the same spirit to create a world of disharmony, disease, and poverty. Spiritual Biology simply means the role of spirit in creating a brilliant mind and healthy body, as they both are essential for us to successfully climb the ladder of evolution. Only man is known to possess the discriminating faculty of thought. By the clear understanding of our reciprocal relationship with the creative spirit, that primordial energy (with which everything is manifested, including ourselves), we can apply the principles of spirit to create a world of our choice instead of a world that the tyrannical circumstances as widely believed have created for us. The supreme Law of Spirit is its transparent harmony as we witness its all-pervading presence throughout the landscape of gratitude. The same is true with our own very nature, which is total harmony and peace—if only we could perceive it.

The Story of the Prodigal Son

The story of the anecdotal prodigal son in the Bible is not a simple story—it is a metaphysical revelation of man's relationship to his maker, the Father who is a symbol of the creative power of the universe. As long as the son (individual man) was with the father, he was enjoying the father's protection and his wealth. But as he strayed away from home (the domain of spirit, the dwelling place of the father), the son not only lost his father's protection—he was also restless, as he was devoid of the empowering sense of harmony which offers a blanket of protective peace (which our innate nature is). It simply means that when we stray away from our innate nature of spirit, we are afflicted by the pangs of separation, which is the root cause of disharmony and disease; this is the principal domain of negativity in the universe. In that sense, we are all the Biblical prodigal sons as we stray from the domain of spirit—the dwelling places of the father—who has given us the gift of external life and the everlasting presence of harmony in the true unmanifested spiritual world. When you know who you are, the evolution is complete as you have no more Everest to climb.

When the prodigal son realized that he had strayed too far from the father (as the creative spiritual wisdom dawned on him), he returned to his father's home (the domain of spirit and the dwelling place of the Divine). His harmony and peace was restored, as nothing else is possible in the presence of the father who is the bestower of peace and tranquility in the universe. Hence the great master and the teacher of spirit taught, "Seek ye first the kingdom of God and its righteousness, and everything shall be added unto you."

The infinite, living, healing presence is all around us, as nothing is created that is not out of spirit; everything is the dwelling place of the eternal spirit, the giver of harmony and peace. All that is required of us is an understanding that everything is spirit, and to honor the harmony of spirit in our thoughts, speech and actions.

> Doubt not, fear not, work on and wait,
> As sure as dawn shall conquer dark,
> So love will triumph over hate,
> And spring will bring lark.
>
> —Douglas Malloch

Yes, we have to eliminate negativity made of doubt and fear, and sincerely work with a fervent faith that everything multiplies after its kind. "Like attracts the like," is a universal law which applies everywhere for everyone, regardless of his race, religion or creed. As Lord Krishna says in Bhagavad Gita, a classic textbook of psychotherapy, "You have the right to work, but not to the fruit thereof." While many educated ones question the statement, it is clear truth that you do not have to demand the fruit of action, as it will be simply given to you. Certain things in life you do not have to demand, such as mother's love and reward for one's actual work. They both are given to you. While you demand work, you do not have to demand the reward, as work includes the reward as proclaimed in the universal law, "everything multiplies after its kind." The moment you grasp the meaning of this universal law, you will recognize the value of hard work, and you will no longer demand the reward for your work. Those who are unhappy at work will realize their own folly; the reward for work is not forthcoming because of their own negative thoughts, as their own negativity affects the quality of work they are producing every day. That negative state of mind is responsible for their own inability to forge ahead in the workplace. It is not the company, nor the supervisor, nor management—it is their own negative state of mind that creates their own limitations. As the Bible puts it, "What I have feared has fallen upon me."

Two thousand years before Jesus Christ appeared in Jerusalem, it was written in Vedas, the sacred text of the Hindus, that if two of us unite in the name of spirit, we can conquer the world, though singly we could not accomplish that great task. Then appeared the Son of God who said that if two of us agree on anything we desire, it shall be done to us. Ordinary calculation tells us that one added to one is only two. But in spirituality, when two psyches pray together, it multiplies several times— not merely twice, as the ordinary arithmetic tells us. The power of spiritual energy is non-measurable, even under the scrutiny of a powerful microscope.

Science, with its marriage to precision and measurements, has a problem with spiritual energy which defies the laws of physics and chemistry. The secret of this amazing multiplying power of spirit lies in the word *catalyst*. In chemistry, the word *catalyst* means an agent or substance which, when added to another chemical, releases as many units of power as the original chemical contains. Thus, when two people unite their spiritual power, each one acts as a catalyst for the other, releasing several times the power that one may possess. When two people unite their thoughts in prayer, the results are amazing.

CHAPTER FOUR

The Miracle of Hard Work

There is a miracle hiding in hard work which I have witnessed throughout the last four decades. I seldom worked forty hours regularly in my career—I always worked fifty to sixty hours a week, and many times my work week exceeded seventy hours. I am convinced that there is a magic in working hard. It guarantees success in whatever field of work you choose to engage in. Your intelligence, education and charisma all will help you when you begin your career, but hard work alone can ensure success and guarantee a steady stream of income. Most of the time, an increasing stream of income will amaze even the most optimistic person in the world. A regular forty hours will help you make a living, but a fifty or sixty hour work week will guarantee the luxury of a discretionary income. I am the beneficiary of discretionary income throughout my life.

There is no substitute for hard work. It is enshrined in the Law of Karma. Every action has its own consequences; hard work has its own Reward. Nobody can take it away from you. The longer it is withheld, the bigger the Reward. The Divine Justice System will make sure that you are paid with compound interest!

I have witnessed the operation of the Law of Karma throughout my working life, spanning almost half a century. I started my career in the accounting department at the age of twenty after finishing my undergraduate degree in accounting. My first paycheck was in Rs 150.00 (rupees) which is equivalent to $30.00 USD (in 1964). It did not discourage me, as I wanted to be employed one day earlier after graduation, not one day later. But within three months of experience with that employer, I changed my job with an income three times higher than my first paycheck. During the next eight years of working in India, I finished my master's degree with a full-time job, and changed my career from accounting to teaching. After a couple of years of teaching experience, I went back to the steel industry as a corporate executive until I emigrated to the United States in 1972. While working in the industry, my average day was much more than eight hours, as an average work week exceeded sixty to seventy hours. Looking back, it was the best thing that ever happened to me. While I was spending almost all my waking hours at work, I was gathering invaluable experience, which helped boost my confidence and enthusiasm as I adjusted to the challenging work atmosphere in the U.S.

My Role Model

My brother, Mr. K.S. Nair (who retired from the Indian government service as director of inspection) was my role model. He was the epitome of hard work and a beacon of hope for everybody around him. He was indeed a self-made man who always embraced the principle of hard work, and it helped him reach the pinnacle of his career when he retired. He highly valued education, and earned his professional certificate in cost accounting as well as a master's degree, all with sheer hard work while employed full-time. I had the privilege of observing him very closely at a young age, and it helped me understand the value of hard work. I owe my appreciation for hard work to my brother alone, and my soul will remain ever indebted to such a great man whose selfless love is the cause of what I am today. It was his close association and guidance that helped me to understand the value of hard work.

Going The Extra Mile

In the Bible, we read about going the extra mile, which is another expression for hard work. It is a privilege to give more work that what you are paid for. Even if you are not paid for those extra hours you put in, think about the experience and the confidence level you attain by putting in more hours. Every employer can use a few more hours from each employee, and it helps the overall productivity of the corporation, which will help improve the bottom line. Increased profits can improve working conditions and a favorable atmosphere for a raise for every employee. Always remember, there is more joy in giving than receiving. In addition to increasing one's confidence level, it also gives a sense of contentment and satisfaction.

A Sound Work Ethic

A sound work ethic is an important ingredient of greater sales achievement. It establishes your love for success, and ultimately it becomes a lifestyle. History is filled with great achievers who worked hard, even when they were not paid nor appreciated for their hard work; however, they all knew the operation of the Law of Karma. Law of Karma, simply put, says:

> If you sow the seeds of oranges, never expect to reap apples.

Every hard work pays. In Bhagavad Geetha, Lord Krishna says, "You have the right to work and not to the fruit thereof." Perform your duty without expectation of the outcome. If you look at this statement, it appears that Lord Krishna is a capitalist who has no heart for the working class. Yet a close analysis of this statement shows that Lord Krishna knew exactly the meaning of the Law of Karma, and He only tried to advance its cause for the benefit of mankind. Let us analyze this statement and understand its spiritual significance.

You have the right to work:

A right is something that you demand, so you demand work and are fully engaged. "An idle mind is a devil's workshop." So Lord Krishna advocates a healthy mind which is always engaged in action. Every field of work contributes to the social benefit or common good of mankind. Thus every single individual who is fully engaged in his or her field of work can make a difference.

Hard work is also an antidote for lethargy, an ailment that affects millions of people around the globe. Think of the global productivity increase if every able-bodied man and woman put in fifty to sixty hours of work every week. The world would be filled with more than enough goods and services for the benefit of everyone. Poverty and starvation would vanish, there would be plenty of food for everyone, and no doubt this world would be a better place to live in. This simple principle of demanding work is a cure-all for all our poverty and starvation. With the abolishment of poverty there will be less violence in the world, and a peaceful society will emerge.

But not to the fruit thereof:

Lord Krishna says to demand work, but not to demand the fruit (the reward) of your action. It is not a capitalistic statement of labor exploitation—it is more than that; it is sincere advice for prosperity and progress.

If you think of the reward for your work, the quality of your work will suffer. So when you work, focus on the work and give it your undivided attention! Devotion, Lord Krishna says, is the secret of quality. We have invested billions of dollars in ensuring the quality of work at corporations manufacturing goods and services, yet we do not spend enough resources to educate the workforce to give its undivided attention to the work. Nothing less than full devotion is acceptable. Preoccupation with the reward for the work distracts from quality, so take away the thought of the fruit of your action while working, and watch everyone's productivity soar.

In my sales career, I have experienced this several times. In 1989, I was working with Metlife as an account executive. A good friend and client referred me to one of his colleagues, another doctor, who wanted to get a mortgage loan. She was told by my friend, "Just talk to Gopi and he will help you."

Even though I was not doing mortgages at that time, I used to refer my clients to Chase Mortgage, which was located across from our office. She and her husband came to my office and got all the documents for the loan, which I then handed over to my friend Tom, the vice president with Chase Mortgage. Since they had good credit and income, the process was accelerated and the loan was ready to close in less than two weeks. When the day of closing came, the doctor could not come for the closing, as she was called in for an emergency. She called me and explained her predicament. I talked to Tom, and we arranged for him to meet closer to the hospital in order to get the closing done. The doctor was not only happy, she was incredulous at what Chase did for her on such short notice.

She called me the following week to thank me, and I said that I was happy for her. But then she said something that amazed me. She said, "Mr. Nair, you spent a lot of time helping me, and you went out of the way to get the closing done in the operating room. I am going to send you a check for $1000.00." I told the doctor that I was honored by her remarks, but that I did not expect her to send me a check as I would have done the same for any of my clients or their referrals. She insisted on sending the check, but I told her that if she did so, I would have to return it to her as it was against my principles. She understood that I meant what I said and agreed not to send the check, but she said thanks several times. We ended the conversation on a very pleasant note.

Seven years later, I received a call from the same doctor who was looking for a Second to Life policy as a part of the estate planning. I made an appointment to meet with her and her husband. After giving her the information, she decided to go with the plan; my income from that transaction was over $10,000. To add a more spice to the Law of Karma, she referred her friend for a similar plan; between the two doctors, I made an income in excess of $20,000.

Now you know why I am a firm believer in the operation of the Law of Karma. If the reward for your action is delayed longer, the Divine Justice System will make sure that you are paid with compound interest. There certainly was a lot of compound interest in that $20,000 commissions check.

My Regular Work Week

After I made my goal for 2012 at $500,000, I knew that I have to have an action plan backed by hard work. My average day looked like this:

Reach office	-	7:00 AM
		6 Hours
Leave office	-	1:00 PM
Return to office	-	4:00 PM
		5.5 Hours
Leave office	-	9:30 PM

I work seven days a week.

Because I am in the office before everybody gets in, I have roughly two hours of quiet time to do my paperwork and make a few telephone calls. In a quiet atmosphere, you can accomplish almost a half day's work in two hours, as you have no distractions. In the evening, after 6:00, I reserve the time to meet clients who are new or who come for their closings. Many times, clients can come after work; the time between 6:00 PM and 9:30 PM makes them feel very comfortable.

Spousal Consent

When you look at my work schedule, you might think that I have no family life as I am in the office most of my waking hours. In my particular case, since my kids are all grown up, I have the luxury of spending long hours in the office. I have an understanding with my wife. Whenever she needs me, I am at home, and if she does not need me, I am at the office. So it is very important for every salesperson to take the spouse into confidence about your long hours at work or meeting with clients outside the office. To compensate for the hardship your spouse goes through, you must find time to spend with him or her and surprise the spouse whenever you can. It is said that behind every successful man there is a woman. It applies to successful women, too. Behind every successful woman, there is the support and confidence of her man. Since salespeople tend to spend a lot more hours in sales activities and travel, the consent of one's spouse is a very necessary ingredient of a successful sales career.

Sales Universe

The Sales Universe is a state of mind. It is embedded in positive thinking, positive speech, and positive action. When you interact with your prospects and clients, you must inspire them with unselfish thoughts. Your words must uplift them and give them a confidence they have never known. Your actions must only enhance their own self-esteem. Regardless of whether or not you do business with them, treat them with respect; your words must bring them sunshine and optimism. You must never discuss or mention your problems with your prospects or clients. They must never hear anything about your office politics. Never criticize your competition, and if a discussion ensues, always talk highly about your competition and other companies in the same business. The truth is that you have no competition; there is nobody like you in the Sales Universe—you are unique and one of a kind. You are always engaged in selling yourself to the prospective client. People want to do business with trustworthy individuals, and with those in whose company they feel valued.

Your Sales Universe is a very kind universe. It is impersonal, and it is an eternal programmer, programmed to give back to you whatever you have offered to the Universe—in fact, several times more. It is the Master of Reciprocity. There is no entity like the Universe which reciprocates in kind; whatever you give, you get back multiplied. Since you are dealing with the Master of Reciprocity, you can expect to get back in kind whatever you offer to your clients—the inhabitants of your Sales Universe.

As Above, So Below

The great Emerald Tablet** proclaimed this thought more than five thousand years ago. This truth is applicable for all human beings, including people who are engaged in sales: "As you think, so you have become." A thorough understanding of this truth will save any salesperson from the phenomenon of sales slumps. Most salespeople experience sales slumps, or a period of decline after super sales accomplishments. Always feed your thoughts with optimism, and never take advantage of any situation. Train yourself to do the right thing for the client, and walk the extra mile in each case.

Now that you know the Law of Karma, you can work for the client and spend hours together, even if they do not do business with you. The efforts you put in will never go unrewarded. You are keeping the Sales Universe indebted to you, and as the Master of Reciprocity, it cannot help but give you your reward in due course.

** http://en.wikipedia.org/wiki/Emerald_Tablet

An "Ungrateful Employer"

Many of my friends make the following statement when I talk about going the extra mile and working more than forty hours: "Gopi, I have an ungrateful employer, or an ungrateful boss. He wants to take advantage of me, and I do not want to fall for it. I am too smart for that."

This is a fallacious conclusion, and it only shows ignorance of the operation of the Law of Karma. The Law of Karma (or the Law of Sowing and Reaping) is a Universal Law; it is an inviolable Law, and nobody is above it. Regardless of who your boss is, or who your employer is, the Law will operate without flaws. The Law itself is impersonal; it has no favorites. Every Universal Law is impersonal. For example, the function of fire is to burn. If you put your hand in the fire, it will burn your hand. Even if it is a two-year-old child, the fire will burn his or her hand. You cannot say that the fire is merciless to burn a two-year-old child. The law simply operates, and it cannot favor a two-year-old or handicapped person.

When you work hard, you are not working for the ungrateful employer or an ungrateful boss. You are offering your hard work to the Universe which will reciprocate in kind but multifold. You can see the Law of Karma in operation everywhere around you. Look at a farmer. He sows the seed of barley, oats, or wheat. He waters his farm, puts down manure, and patiently waits for four to six months. He gets a bountiful harvest—many times what he has sown. Once you grasp this secret of sowing and reaping, you will never worry about an ungrateful employer or an ungrateful boss. Many times, an ungrateful boss is the product of one's own negative thoughts—a figment of one's own imagination. Even if your hard work is not acknowledged by your immediate boss or employer, keep on doing it. Since your reward cannot be withheld forever, if you continue to work hard, the Divine Justice System will transplant you from an uninspiring environment to an inspiring environment, and a new employer will be able to make a difference with your talent.

Service With A Smile

Every salesperson must remember that selling is nothing but service with a smile. It is the service factor that makes every salesman a success or failure. Every product or service that a salesman sells is opening the door of opportunity to render prompt and efficient services to one's customers. As a matter of fact, every sale is a service in disguise. We are proposing a product (either tangible or intangible) to a client to solve one of his or her problems. Thus we are all in the problem-solving business and we must always be aware of that fact that the sale is beyond dollars and cents. While we all make a comfortable living being successful in sales, it is only a by-product of our activities. If you look at any of the successful salespersons, you will realize without any doubt that they all serve their customers very well. Thus an attitude to serve is the passport to success for every salesperson. The earlier you learn this secret of success, the better it will be.

Many times, after a service or product is sold, salespeople feel reluctant to spend more time with the client. That is a self-defeating choice. Many times, a customer goes through buyer's remorse. This is an opportunity to cement the relationship, as the customer feels the warmth of your personality and that you are with him/her whenever needed. Every salesperson has to be a good counsellor, a good psychotherapist,t and a very good friend who is willing and able to serve the clients' needs.

A good database of your loyal clients, who will refer their friends and relatives, is the dream of every salesperson. But behind the fulfillment of this dream, there is a lot of sweat. You can do it easily over a period of time if you embrace service with a smile as a sales goal. Just like you monitor your sales activities, you must monitor your service activities, too. It is your willingness and ability to serve your clients that sets you apart from the pack of hundreds of thousands of salespeople who inhabit the Sales Universe.

Here is a sample of a work week for a salesperson with a young family and small children.

Monday–Friday	8:00 AM–6:00 PM	=	10 hours x 5	=	50
Saturday	8:00 AM–2:00 PM	=	6 hours x 1	=	6
Sunday	No Work Total	=	56 hours		

While the time you begin work and end your work day is flexible, you must work at least fifty hours a week to achieve greater sales success. In these days of cellphones, laptops and iPods, communication is so easy and fast that you can even work from home a few hours every week. This will definitely add to your sales revenue. One thing I have noticed is that you will have time for everything, including family time, when you work fifty to sixty hours a week. You become a master of time management, and many of the time wastages (like idle and unnecessary T.V. time) gets eliminated. You will spend time effectively with family as it becomes quality time.

Whenever I think that sales activities are a bit slow, I call my prospects and clients. At the end of the day, it is heartening to note that I called fifty to seventy of my clients, and many of them are happy that I called. All these calls produce sales activities which ultimately end up in sales. Once every three months, I try to call all my clients just to say hello, and they all like it. It is a good sales strategy to be in touch with your clients.

Maintain the work week

Regardless of the state of the economy or other external factors, we must work our forty to fifty plus hours on a regular basis.

This is the only thing on which we have absolute control, and we should not lose focus of our commitment. It is a sacred commitment that we must all uphold, regardless of what external factors influence us. This is a solemn responsibility, and every salesperson must take it very seriously. The weekly working hours can be plotted something like this:

MON	8:00 AM - 6:00 PM	=	10 hours
TUES	8:00 AM - 5:00 PM	=	9 hours
WED	8:00 AM - 6:00 PM	=	10 hours
THURS	8:00 AM - 6:00 PM	=	10 hours
FRI	8:00 AM - 5:00 PM	=	9 hours
SAT	8:00 AM - 2:00 PM	=	6 hours
		TOTAL HOURS	**54**

Keeping score is very important for every salesperson. It is a test of self-discipline; it will encourage all our activities. If you constantly maintain this work schedule, you do not have to worry about your income. It will keep on swelling year after year. Every salesperson will have unexpected emergencies or other demands on their time. We do not have to feel bad about it as it is a part of our life. Do not feel guilty if those personal emergencies cause the hours to drop. Monitoring one's weekly work schedule is the most effective tool against sales slumps. I closely monitor my weekly work schedule to make sure that I work between fifty to sixty hours every week; during the last twenty-five years, I have not experienced any sales slumps.

Avoid Gossip

Avoid gossip at all costs. Negative talk about the economy, one's employer, and other sales professionals must be avoided at all times. The best way to do that is to select your confidantes and friends from the field of sales. With those inspiring friends around you, your tendency to gossip can be curtailed. There will be less repetitive talk about external factors. With the advent of technology, information is spreading like wildfire, and most of it is unfortunately negative and heartbreaking. More information is lethal for every salesperson if it is not selective. Sometimes, less is better.

During the Great Depression, the negative news of the economy was spreading, and people were getting this news through newspapers. At this time, there was a hotdog vendor in New York City. He used to open his business at 5:30 AM and make hotdogs and soft drinks for his customers. He was selling hotdogs at very low price, and his customers surrounded him until he closed his business at 8:00 PM. Even though businesses were closing down everywhere, our hotdog vendor had a very booming business. The reason? He did not read newspapers, because he did not know how to read.

In the modern age, information is overwhelming, and every salesperson must regulate the way they receive and process information on a daily basis. Before you start your day in the morning, do not read negative news. When you turn on the computer, if there is negative news, try not to read it; you can delete or bypass it. Even if you read it, do not dwell on it; you can prevent it from internal absorption. An awareness of the need to refrain from dwelling on negative news is the key to staying positive.

How to Process Information

We are all CPUs—central processing units. An optimistic view of life and cultivating imagination of a positive outcome in every situation is a key to greater sales success. The best way to process any information on a positive note is to train yourself to do so. What happens in life is immaterial, but how you process that information is pivotal to maintaining a positive attitude. Somebody else's experience need not be your experience, so whenever you get any kind of negative news, acknowledge it by saying, "I am grateful for this experience."

The moment you acknowledge an experience with gratitude, you are ready to deal with the situation positively. Gratitude, as we discussed before, is the greatest magic wand, as it can erase negativity. A mind devoid of negativity is a creative mind, and it can process information in a positive way. Sometimes people say that certain information cannot be processed positively because of its negative implications. That is not true. Wherever there is negativity, there is positivity, as both represent the two sides of the same coin. Anything which is negative can be viewed as positive, if you have trained your mind to do so.

Stay Inspired

This is an important step towards avoiding sales slumps. We salespeople must stay inspired at all times. Include in your daily routine the reading of a passage from the scriptures of the Holy Bible, Holy Bhagavad Geetha, Holy Quran, or the Holy Talmud. Reading it internalizes the spiritual meaning and incorporates it in your daily behavior. Reciting scriptures like a parrot without living it is like having a beautiful automobile while still walking everywhere on foot.

You can also have inspirational tapes or CDs that you can keep in your car. Whenever you are in the car, you can play the CD and listen to the inspirational message.

Secret of Staying Inspired

According to my research and observation, the best way to stay inspired is to inspire others. Every salesperson must be inspirational; by thought, speech and deeds, we must strive to inspire one and all who come into contact with us on a daily basis. This must be the silent mission of all people engaged in sales. There is a lot of negativity in this world; if every salesperson makes a commitment to inspire others who come into contact with him or her, this world will definitely become a better place to live.

This has been my silent mission during the last three decades. I am happy to report that it has not only improved my sales, but it has definitely made me a better person. Our thoughts, words and speech, along with our other expressions, must be only to inspire and uplift. We can definitely make a difference in our Sales Universe.

All these steps described above can eliminate Sales Slumps in every salesperson's life. Staying focused, monitoring your work week schedule, avoiding gossip, and staying inspired at all times can make even an ordinary salesperson a sales star, as these comprise the foundation of our Sales Universe. They steep in us self-discipline, without which even the smartest salesperson will be doomed in the sea of frustration and failure. You can live your dreams if you dare to make your knowledge a daily habit.

Transforming negativity into positivity

I received the sad news that my mother had died when my brother-in-law called me in the morning on December 12, 2005. I asked him to tell my brothers not to wait for me to conduct the funeral, as any delay would prolong the agony of my family. I was in a state of confusion for the next two days as I paced back and forth in the kitchen each morning. I was very close to my mother, and I felt guilt that I could not be with her when she departed. *Now that she is gone, what is the purpose of going to India?* I asked myself. The rituals and other ceremonies for the dead, I always thought, were to comfort the living.

There was nothing I could do to bring her back to life. A feeling of guilt, coupled with a feeling of helplessness, darkened my state of mind. Then I began to think outside of myself. *If I am depressed and in a state of helplessness, so are my brothers and my only sister in India,* I realized. I started thinking about my siblings and their suffering, and in a flash, it occurred to me that I could alleviate their suffering. I decided to catch the next plane; my sole mission was to make a difference for my family. I went to India and participated in the rituals for the dead—but more than that, I brought laughter to the home; before my arrival, there was only graveyard silence. I also reminded everybody that our mother always wanted all of us to be happy. We were not gathering there to mourn her death, I said, but to celebrate her life, as Mother is always immortal.

There is a beacon of hope in every tragedy. When you remove your selfish intent from the situation, you can see light at the end of the tunnel. When you live for yourself, life is miserable, but when you live for others, it is pure joy.

Whenever you process any negative information, your focus should be away from your selfish interest. Then you can find the solution hiding in the problem. From disorder emerges order, from disharmony emerges harmony, and from negativity emerges positivity!

CHAPTER FIVE

The Magic of Setting Goals

Introduction to Goal Setting

An arrow of an aim narrows your sorrow
Brings many successes and a worthy tomorrow.

One unwavering aim is all that takes to be successful in life—no matter what calling you choose. Once, a friend asked Michaelangelo, the famous artist and sculptor, "Why do you lead such a solitary life?" He replied, "Art is a jealous mistress; she requires the whole man." It shows how committed he was, and it also points to the secret of his success. Anybody who has been successful in any field of endeavor has had a definite chief aim in life, and with perseverance, all obstacles were surmounted.

A man who wavers and has no definite purpose in life attains no measurable success. Dissipation of thought energy on too many things is the cause of all human failure. All great men of history possessed this great power of concentration, the undivided attention, the one pointedness in their field of endeavor. The famous Victor Hugo, who wrote *The Hunchback of Notre*

Dame in 1930, did not want to be disturbed, even though bullets were flashing across his garden during the revolution. He locked himself in a room in another to avoid any temptation of distraction. In this way, he accomplished the great task of completing a classic work of literature; it is an example of pure concentration.

The fallacy of man knowing many different vocations is very well depicted in the famous story of the cat and the fox. One day, a cat and a fox met on the jungle path. They stopped a while for an chat.

The fox asked the cat, "What will you do to escape if a hunter spots you now?"

"I will climb the top of this tree and hide there until he leaves the jungle," said the cat. "What will you do to escape?" asked the cat of the fox.

"I am not like you," said the fox. "I can run fast to escape, or I can hide in this hole, or I may even attack the hunter."

While they were talking, a hunter came, and the cat disappeared into a tree. While the fox was thinking about what to do, the hunter got him very easily. The moral of the story is to have one definite aim rather than many half-baked aims.

A person with one talent, if he or she concentrates on that, can accomplish greater tasks than a person with ten talents, as he or she dissipates his or her energy a little bit on each of them. Therefore it is essential to find a vocation of your choice, one that you thoroughly enjoy, and concentrate all the energy for the development of that trade or vocation.

The annals of human achievements have been filled with the names of great men who accomplished great things. The great inventors like Edison, Morse, Bell or Howe had one thing in common: they all had a purpose in life, and they gave their life to this one purpose without dissipating energy in all the four directions. Adam Smith spent ten years of dedicated labor to complete the famous book *Wealth of Nations,* while Gibbon gladly dedicated twenty years of his life to complete the book *Decline and Fall of the Roman Empire.* Webster spent thirty-six years to finish the world famous *Webster's Dictionary*, and *History of the United States* was finished only in twenty-six years by Bancroft. There are numberless cases of such devotion to work by champions in the fields of art, science, politics and philosophy.

There is an old proverb that states, "A master of one trade will support a wife and seven children, and a master of seven cannot support himself." How true it is that a "Jack Of All Trades" will travel on the road of mediocrity, while the master of one will travel on the royal route of perfection to embrace success. It is the man with a single aim that always succeeds.

Definition of a Goal

A goal is a burning desire propelled by a commitment to complete the task. Even a weaker soul will act like a man possessed when he has set for himself a definite, chief aim. Every goal is a track to run on; it is a dream to be translated into reality; it is a seed that sprouts in the womb of future. A goal is a burning desire committed to writing.

Ask for More

I bargained with fate for a copper
And fate gladly gave me a copper.
However hard I worked everyday, at the end
I got no more than a copper for wages.
Fate is an honest master, giving just wages
Just what I asked for as priced for my labor
One day in a dream, I saw my master giving gold

To my friend, for the same day's work as I did.
The next day, I worked very hard for my master
And asked for gold as my wages at day's end.
To my astonishment, he handed over to me a gold coin
With a smile and a comment, "You get what you ask for!"

Importance of Goal Setting

Goals give direction in life

A goal is a track to run on; it is a path to follow for every worthwhile accomplishment. A man without a goal is like a ship in the high seas with its rudder broken. It will expend the same fuel as necessary to reach the shore in going round and round as it has lost the sense of direction. It is like a dog trying to catch its own tail. As it goes on spinning and spinning, it gets nowhere. If you don't know the direction or do not have a specific purpose, you reach nowhere. Thousands of young men and women go through life without accomplishing anything, not because they have no talent, but because they have not set any worthwhile goals.

Goals are guideposts in life—they not only give you direction, but they help to preserve the excitement and charm in life. Imagine that you do a day's work only so you can pay all the bills and buy bread to stay alive. You will soon lose charm in life. It will be a reign of monotony, and lethargy will soon set in. We all ride on our ego; one accomplishment after another keeps us going with the business of life. Goals are actually carriers of our ego, taking it from one point in life to another in search of success.

The great Napoleon Hill, the world-renowned author of *Think and Grow Rich*, studied the lives of five hundred highly successful businessmen and women of America. The purpose of his research was to discover common denominations of success, personality traits that they all shared as successful human beings in their field of endeavor. Hill discovered two predominant characteristics common to all those men and women. First of all, they all possessed a high degree of sex drive, meaning they all had exuberant energy, the symbol of sex and love. Secondly, Napoleon Hill also discovered that they all knew what they wanted out of life. They all had written down goals to guide them.

Remove Fear of Change

Change is the essential fabric of life. Every day brings changes in our physical, mental and spiritual spheres of life. If you have any doubt about change, look into the mirror and see how your own physical features have undergone radical changes over the years. In fact, life itself is a parade of changes, from infancy to early childhood, to adulthood to old age, before we wither away to join the elements. We are all afraid of change because of the uncertainties associated with it. The moment you know what is going to happen tomorrow, the day after, and in the future, the fear is gone. In other words, we as human beings do not relish the unpredictability of the future. The age-old practice of going to fortune tellers and soothsayers clearly reveals this aversion and fear towards change.

What is Fear?

F—Fictitious
E—Experience
A—Acting
R—Real

Fear is the deadliest of all emotions. It is silent and fatal if unchecked or not managed properly. The more you think of fear, the more strength it gathers to destroy you. Every fear is a fictitious experience; we give it form and strength to make it appear very real. There is no reality other than perception, and if you perceive fear to be real, it will prove to be real. It is only in your perception that a post looks like a ghost in the night, and a rope looks like a snake in darkness.

Goals help us remove the fear of change, because we know exactly what we want to do and how it should be accomplished. Even if unexpected difficulties arise, we are prepared to solve them with organized effort. It is said that obstacles are what you see when you take your mind off the goal. Goals indeed help us focus our attention and energy towards the accomplishment of a given task at any time. Time and talent is not worth wasting on worthless fears.

Chart the Course of the Future

Life is a cluster of memories. Every day, we weave the fabric of dreams, bringing new experiences to enrich life. A great purpose adds meaning and purpose. Our everyday efforts are directed towards the accomplishment of our written goal. These small deeds, performed on a daily basis, chart the course of a bright future. As we tread the waters of life with goals as our guide-posts, we enlighten and enrich our life, bringing not only joy to ourselves, but those around us. As the summer of happiness blooms, the winter of sorrow and frustration withers away.

Improve the Quality of Life

As we add discipline to life, we enjoy living. The quality of life depends upon purpose and meaning. Goals improve the quality of our daily life, and we no longer live for creature comforts alone. We look beyond our own limited sphere and envision the happiness of the family, the community, the country, and finally the world at large. As we expand the horizon of our vision, we encompass the whole of human consciousness far and beyond our limited being. We care for others, and their wellbeing becomes a matter of great concern to us. When we try for the wellbeing and happiness of others, we will be showered with joy and happiness as we have never experienced before. Goals, worthwhile goals, indeed improve the quality of life.

Always remember, life is as transient as dew drops dancing on one's palms. It is here in this moment; in the next moment it may or may not. All earthly things belong to Mother Earth, no matter how successful one is. No one can take anything with him when he finally departs. In fact, we own nothing; we have temporary use of things in this world. When the end comes, even the loved ones stand back and weep helplessly. Man is a traveler from the cradle to the graveyard. Our external companions are nothing but our deeds. Goals help us to perform good deeds, deeds that not only bring happiness to us, but others as well.

Multiply Financial Rewards

It is said that people who have no goals will work for people who have set their own goals. Now, you decide if you want to work for others all your life or set your own goals to climb the ladder of meaningful achievement. While money alone is not the measure of success, a person with money can do a lot of things, not only for himself, but for others around him. Great philanthropists of the world have amassed wealth in industry and science, and towards the end of their lives, they distributed their wealth between their loved ones and the extended family of humankind. You too can leave a legacy of compassion and care if you have been successful and have amassed wealth. Wealth is good, desirable, and covetable, as long as it brings joy to others.

At Yale University, people did a study of the graduating class of 1953 as to their goal-setting habits. Of all the students who graduated in 1953, only three percent had set any goals in life. Twenty years later, the research team followed up with the class of 1953 to see how well they were doing financially. To their surprise, they discovered that the three percent of students who had goals surpassed the income of the ninety-seven percent of students that had no goals. What an amazing discovery. So it is quite true that financial rewards can be multiplied by setting worthwhile goals and following them closely to as they are seen through to their accomplishment.

The importance of goal-setting cannot be overlooked. Goals not only help you to drive away the devils from the doorsteps of your mind, they help you grow to your full potential. It is the spiritual fertilizer for human growth and achievement. They are friendly reminders they help us to realize our full potential. As the great Saint Swami Vivekananda said, "Every human is a potential divine." You and I carry in us the sparks of divinity. Goals act as the fuel to keep this divinity glowing with accomplishment after accomplishment to realize our full potential.

Reasons for Not Goal Setting

Not realizing the importance of setting goals

More than ninety-five percent of people go through life without any plan for growth and achievement. They go to work to earn money to buy bread so they can go to work again. Most of us are afflicted by mediocrity with no room for excellence.

Most of the valuable lessons in life we learn from our parents, as they are very close to us during the formative years of our life. If parents are not exposed to ideas of goal-setting, there is no way they are going to bring them out during a family discussion. It is very likely that children of parents who have set their own goals have a higher probability of having their own goals.

People often do not set goals because they do not realize the importance of doing so. Elementary schools, high schools, and even colleges do not impart any instruction in goal-setting. There could be very limited cases of certain teachers inspiring students to uplift their potential. There are also cases such as the gifted child program where a group of teachers work together with above-average students to brings up their potential. Beyond that, there is no set program to train students at any level of instruction in the art of goal-setting.

I envision a world where boys and girls at a young age—as early as eight or nine years old—are introduced to the art of goal-setting at home as well as in schools. When they are fixed on a noble purpose or an unwavering aim, the whole world will be a dazzling sight of great human achievements. Possessed by the spirit of achievement with goals set up to guide through the terrains of achievements, that youth is bound to win the world and will find a way to accommodate it. When this world is endowed with such souls of resolve, it will be an awesome sight to watch the pillars of civilization supporting every corner of this planet. They will challenge every opposition; every obstacle will be scaled back as a stepping stone, no matter what appears on the way. Their eyes will be fixed on their goals like a beast gazing at its prey.

No Training in Goal Setting

Boys and girls going through high school education do not get even an hour of instruction in the art of goal-setting. The curriculum prescribed for a high school diploma is important to provide the stimulus necessary to bring out the potential of the hidden sprit in every breathing mortal. Those entrusted with the task of coaching our young men and women themselves may not have had any exposure to the art of goal setting. Therefore, any help from the last generation of teachers is like expecting a harvest from a barren land.

Coming to institutions of higher learning like colleges and universities, the situation is no different than high schools. Most of them do not offer even an hour of training in goal setting. They tend to have shown some changes lately as some of the schools have broken the deadly pattern of no training to some such training. This, coupled with contributions from the great stalwarts in the motivational arenas like Brian Tracy, Robert Schuller, and the late Dr. Norman Vincent Peale, has added some hope to the cause of training youngsters and executives in setting goals.

It is the author's dream that by the year 2020, at least a few hundred if not a thousand goal setting clinics should be conducted to whip up the awareness. Though it is an outlandish dream, any such move to involve the high schoolers will be nothing less than spectacular, even if it means hours and hours of relentless effort. The high schoolers for us represent the torch bearers of the future. Those fertile minds sown with the seeds of noble goals will be the only salvations from this world torn apart with racial and religious unrest along with the narrow walls of separation no matter on what basis they are erected. Helping them to expand the horizon of their vision with noble ideals spearheaded by universal love and kindness will undoubtedly create a future generation of considerate human beings willing to gladly to share this planet with their fellow travelers in their journey to the temple of eternity. Peace and harmony with reign in their hearts, cooperation will dictate their survival instincts and love and understanding will replace the hatred that wrecks the very civilization that brought us the annals of human endeavor.

A journey of a thousand miles starts with one step, and several baby steps that we take in creating awareness will strengthen the cause of goals. All the participants in this noble task of creating a homogeneous awareness can feel heartened that one day, this world will be filled with people with lofty ideals and worthwhile goals to enrich their lives and the loved ones around them.

More and more people will begin to set goals as the level of awareness and training in techniques begins to accelerate. High schools and colleges will bristle with activities directed towards perfecting techniques of goal setting, and boys and girls will start charting the course of their destiny before they enter adult life. The privileged few who have goals today will be replaced by the majority who spend time and energy to decide their future roles rather than letting it be shaped by the ruthless hands of a tyrant fate.

> *In idle wishes, fools find paradise*
> *But the wise choose to exert before their demise*
> *Life's rewards await those who have written goals*
> *Surely, they are the ones who will carve out their roles.*

Fear of Rejection

Another cardinal reason why most of the people do not set goals is the fear of rejection. Fears of rejection can be very well understood by understanding the joy of acceptance. We all like to be accepted by our dear ones at home, by our peers at our place of work, and by fellow human beings in society in general. The level of self-confidence a person displays is directly proportional to the level of acceptance enjoyed. Conversely, the degree of self-doubt a person suffers is directly proportional to the fear of rejection he imagines. In fact, fear of rejection is a major cause of many people refraining from setting worthwhile goals.

For example, if I announce to my family that I set my financial goal at $100,000.00 a year, and my wife laughs at me and ridicules me for such an outlandish and unattainable goal, my enthusiasm will shrink like a deflated balloon. As a result, I will be afraid of rejection, and remain a member of the pack of mediocrity without ever trying to set goals.

The pain inflicted by the fear of rejection is excruciating, especially when it comes from people who are close, like members of the family or intimate friends or associates. So we all take the easy route, going through the motions of living, never bothering to be extraordinary. We conclude that if we stay mediocre, then nobody will make fun of us for having outlandish dreams, for reaching for the moon.

At a later stage in this book, we will discuss in detail people with whom we should discuss our personal goals. Suffice it (for now) to say that we should keep our goals confidential, and never discuss them—not even with a spouse, that is, if she (or he) is not supportive of your dreams and goals. Any negative comment or rejection coming from a loved one will throw you off, and your dreams and goals will be shattered.

On the contrary, in a family where father, mother, and children all set goals in their own respective ways, it will be fun to have the goals discussed openly, as family support will add clout to the individual's efforts. Most successful people come out of such understanding families, and even when one member has a tough time, others will offer maximum support and cooperation.

If you do not see positive people around you, make them positive by your own positive behavior. A positive mental attitude, or an attitude of expectation, is mandatory to personal achievement and growth. Fear of rejection, however—the major cause of not setting goals—is bred out of self-doubt and lack of self-confidence.

Reject the fear of rejection; remove the cobwebs of self-doubt; with unshaken faith in one's own ability to ascend to higher altitudes, it is possible to overcome this fatal fear. Like any other fear, it sprouts in one's mind. Rejection takes firm roots as you dwell over it again and again; nip it in the bud—do not brood over the fear. Refrain from giving it form and strength, and you shall overcome this tyrant that has wrecked the bright future of millions and millions of people all over the world.

Muster your strength, and examine the annals of human history wherein lies the stones of radiant stalwarts of politics, industry, and science whose ideas were initially rejected by society. Look to those who stood with conviction, against all odds, as they worked to win the acclaim from the very society that rejected them. Many of them received their recognition posthumously, years after their departure from this world. Take the example of Jesus Christ who was ridiculed; his teachings were rejected as blasphemy by the so-called elders of that time. Today, those very teachings bring solace, comfort and peace to billions of people over the world. Think about it. If your ideas are rejected, and if your goals are rejected as ridiculous by your loved ones or close associates, rejoice. You are in good company.

Fear of Failure

Another reason why people do not set goals is because of the fear of failure. It is safe to say that most of us have tasted the bitterness of failure. Those failed experiences add fuel to our feelings of fear when we undertake any greater tasks. When the phantoms of fears trespass into the chambers of your heart and weaken your spirit, all the dreams that you secretly cherish in your bosom fly out the window.

The truth about fear is that it is a fictitious, imaginary experience that appears to be very real. Most fears are unfounded; the fearful scenarios which we imagine rarely come to pass, and if they do, it is the exception rather than the rule. When those rare events occur, nobody can do anything about it. The best way to manage one's fear is to understand it and substitute fear thoughts with positive, uplifting thoughts.

Manage fears successfully, and turn negative feelings into positive by cultivating faith in oneself and in the higher power of which we are all a potential.

What is Faith?

| F | - | Feelings |
| A | - | Affecting |

I	-	Individuals'
T	-	Thought
H	-	Habits

Day by day, in every way, weave together goodness, kindness, compassion, and so on with your thoughts in order to form the very fabric of habit. We are all slaves of habit, so if you have to be a slave, why not become the slave of good habits? Think good thoughts; make it a task of your daily routine, like brushing your teeth and taking a shower. If you don't take the time to cultivate good and happy thoughts, bad thoughts will take root in your mind to make you a lifelong slave. Believe me, habit is a merciless master. Even those who boast of their willpower do not realize the deadly grip of habit on their life.

We should learn to experience failures. There is a difference between experiencing failure in a certain field and becoming a total failure. Thomas A. Edison, the greatest inventor the world, had more than a thousand patents to his credit, and failed ten thousand times before he perfected the incandescent light bulb. After five thousand times of failure, a young reporter approached him and asked, "Mr. Edison, are you not wasting your time and energy? After five thousand times, your experiments with the electric bulb have failed." The great inventor, who not only was a great scientist but a master of metaphysics, said, "Young man, you do not understand. I have successfully identified five thousand times things that do not work." What incredible self-confidence faith this genius possessed!

School of Adversity

The greatest school in this world is the school of adversity; it is far better than Harvard, MIT, Yale and Princeton. Any young person graduating from the school of adversity is a winner, a hero who has successfully subdued the tyranny of failure. Thousands of young men and women with untold talents are lost to the world every day because they have not been challenged by the obstacles of poverty and adversity. It has been said that the toughest steel is forged in the hottest fire; so also a young man or a woman growing up in adversity has the fortitude to face day-to-day obstacles as they march towards success.

Fools are exasperated by adversity while the wise and the courageous ones welcome them. The famous English poet Byron was ruthlessly criticized for his first book *Hours of Idleness* which was published when he was in his teens. Stung by determination to rise to the top, his slumbering faculties responded, and he stood amongst the top English poets in a few years. All of the greatest men of the world were raised from humble beginnings. They were well-educated, as most of them graduated from the school of adversity. The great city of London rose like a phoenix after it had been burnt down by a massive fire, and after a deadly plague ran through its length and breadth claiming a hundred thousand lives. Even today, the city of London is a tourist attraction putting on display its dazzling past enriched by the English royalty.

There is a genius hidden in every human being, like an angel imprisoned in every marble block. The sculptor dreams of the angel, and his imagination brings the best out of the marble block. Mother Nature is a sculptor, mercilessly chipping and pounding us to wake up the sleeping giant of a scientist or an industrialist or an artist. Those who have the stamina and power of endurance to withstand her merciless pounding in the school of adversity become great in their chosen field of endeavor, leaving their legendary footprints on the sands of time for generations to follow. So welcome every admission to the school of adversity; it will bring out the best in you.

Goal of Goal Setting

The goal of goal setting is to impregnate the subconscious mind

Goal setting impresses the subconscious mind—that layer beneath the conscious mind, which is the seat of emotion. When impressed, anything is possible. Every single step in our goal-setting practice invokes the power of the subconscious mind. To understand the unlimited power of the subconscious mind, we must take a glance at the very organization of the human mind in order to grasp its role in the cognitive process and beyond.

The Greatest Discovery

"That's one small step for man, one giant leap for mankind," said astronaut Neil Armstrong as he departed from his spacecraft and took his first step on the Moon. Mankind has made rapid progress in the realm of physical science, from splitting atoms to sending a man to the Moon; today, many more discoveries are in progress. The advancement of science and technology has indeed improved our standard of living, and with the advent of computers and the age of information, ideas can traverse back and forth at the blink of an eye. If you think this is the best that humankind can accomplish, wait for the next decade and beyond as we embark on an era of development in the realm of mental science. As we have entered the twenty-first century, physical science has marched from glory to glory, but we have not even scratched the surface of the science of the mind. In spite of the rapid increase of material advancement, our capacity to enjoy life has been steadily decreasing, while unrest and a lack of peace and harmony increases.

The secret of the ages is in the discovery of one's own slumbering power, buried deep within the subconscious mind. All the great men and women of science, industry, art and politics have stumbled upon it, whether intentionally or unintentionally; you too can discover this stupendous power, harnessing its energy for everyday use in order to redirect your life.

There is an "inner power" or an "inner urge" in each and every one of us, prompting us towards ever-increasing achievements. At one time or the other, we all have experienced this inner prompting. These are whispers from eternity, which is your own inner self trying to communicate to you. This intuitive voice of wisdom is our counsel, our friend and advisor, and will take us from one glory to another. Trust your instinct or intuition; it has a message for you.

This same intuitive voice sent Columbus across the ocean, transformed Thomas Edison from a farm boy to an inventive genius of the century, and drove Henry Ford from being a poor auto mechanic at the age of forty to become the richest man in the world at the age of sixty. This is the same voice that is telling you that, at some released moment, you can do anything you wish, and you can be anybody you wish. This inner voice is the driving force of all human achievements.

Understanding the power of the subconscious mind, using that inborn power to guide your everyday life, and enabling you to be in touch with that stupendous power is the sum and substance of goal setting. Those ritual practices and exercises in one way or another help us to be in line with the hidden powers of our subconscious mind.

Organization of a Human Mind

Conscious Mind	-	*Choosing Mind*
Subconscious Mind	-	*Obeying Mind*
Super Conscious Mind	-	*Absorbing Mind*

Conscious Mind

The conscious mind is the mind with which we all are familiar; it is the mind that governs the five senses. When I say, "I am hungry," it is my conscious mind that is saying this. It is the discriminative mind choosing between right and wrong; it is the rational mind reasoning out its choices; it is the planning mind planning your family, finances and vacations. It reasons out with logical thinking. Logical thinking is the major attribute of the conscious mind. This is also the mind with which you focus, concentrate and plan your current and future life.

If you compare our life to a movie, the role of the conscious mind is that of the movie director who is entrusted with the task of coordinating and harmonizing every aspect of that particular movie. The success of a movie depends upon the talent of the director, his ability to visualize things in minute detail as a panorama of events, and his insistence on a superior-quality performance. The success of every individual depends upon his ability to use the conscious mind to enlist the support of the other deeper faculties that slumber beneath the surface, converting those "paranormal" forces into normal powers for everyday use.

The conscious mind should be the watchman at the gate of our mind, deciding what impressions or thoughts should go in, and what should not be allowed entry. It is to this conscious mind the subconscious looks for all it impressions. In whatever way the conscious mind (the director) directs, the subconscious mind simply obeys without any question or resistance, because the latter is only an all-obeying servant of the conscious mind. The stability and vision of the conscious mind is the prerequisite for success in any branch of life. A conscious mind consumed by fear, worry and anxiety cannot direct other faculties effectively; as a result, it solidifies the statement, "What I have feared has fallen upon me."

The most important function of the conscious mind is to center the thoughts on things you want, and to remove the thoughts from things you don't want. Always keep your thoughts focused on health, wealth, happiness and harmony, not only for you, but for all those around you, regardless of their relationship to you. Do not dwell on sickness, poverty, hatred, lust and other negative qualities; you do not want to see them realized in your life. As Emile Coue said, "The conscious can put the subconscious mind over the hurdles."

The conscious mind is also known as the active mind, the objective mind and the male mind (denoting its dominance over the subconscious). This mind also enjoys the faculty of discrimination. The major difference between man and the beast is in the power of discrimination. While the man is endowed with the power of discrimination, the beast is deprived of it. For example, a dog walks onto your beautifully kept lawn, and you give the dog a blow. It cries and runs away. Tomorrow, it can make an appearance on your lawn, forgetting the experience of the day before. But if you go to your neighbor's house and he insults you, you will never walk into his house unless he apologizes. This is your faculty of discrimination at work.

The conscious mind can also be called the master mind—the mind that directs and gives orders to the subconscious mind. One of the salient objectives of mental science is to train us to use the conscious mind as a guide or a guardian angel at the gate of our mind. Awareness is our trusted watchman, searching every thought craving entrance for its suitability or eligibility before granting entry into the secret realm of our mind's sphere.

The Subconscious Mind

Do you know how much water, salt, iron or phosphorous you must have in your bloodstream to maintain a specific gravity in your ordinary daily life? How much you should increase the chemicals if you are going to play a game of tennis or work out for an hour? How many glasses of water you should drink to dilute the excess salt you took in from the canned food you ate?

Rejoice if you don't know the answers to the above questions. It is all calculated for you by the subconscious mind, which works faster than any computer. It moves faster than a spacecraft, and it can transcend time and space in time of need. When you go to sleep, suspending the sense organs, your heart is beating, hair and nails are growing, the cells are getting repaired, and digestive processes are going on. All of these are attended to in a minute detail by the all-knowing subconscious mind.

Our subconscious mind is faster than any lightning-fast calculator. It can humble any Nobel Prize-winning mathematician or chemist in its ability to calculate and affect changes at a moment's notice. It is the power of the subconscious that governs digestion, assimilation, excretion, and secretion of which we are not aware, except to know that it is all going on as smoothly as a symphony. The subconscious mind has the power not only to keep you in perfect health, but to endow you with anything you want in life, whether it is riches, fame, or the ability to sing or perform any physical feats.

THE IGNORANCE OF THE POWER OF THE SUBCONSCIOUS MIND TO GOVERN OUR AFFAIRS, whether PERSONAL, BUSINESS OR SPIRITUAL, IS THE CAUSE OF ALL OUR FAILURES IN LIFE.

It is the subconscious mind that heals the body and keeps it in good health.

It transcends time and space to gather information.

It is the seat of emotions.

It is the abode of paranormal faculties like telepathy, clairvoyance, psychokinesis, etc.

It is the giver of intuition.

Premonition is its attribute.

It warns of impending danger and causes you to perform stupendous physical feats.

It is always pro-life—meaning to serve and preserve not to destroy it.

It can facilitate the meeting between minds and meeting with the super-conscious, all-absorbing mind, the resting place of all movements.

It is a very powerful benevolent force, but like any other force, it could be destructive if you do not understand the laws governing this force.

Anything we say or do with an emotionally-charged voice or nerves, the subconscious mind translates into a reality by giving its physical forms. A Michael Jordan, a Babe Ruth or a Nancy Kerrigan, by their relentless practice in the physical art or sport they choose, have been only harmonizing the powers of the subconscious mind by constantly impressing their intentions upon it. Practice is the art of imprisoning the subconscious mind. Anything that is impressed on the subconscious mind will do anything necessary to make it a reality.

Law of the Subconscious

The law of belief is the law of the subconscious mind. When the great master said, "Whatsoever you shall pray and ask for, believe you have received, and you shall receive," he was only laying down a fundamental rule of mental science. Even the principle of the Trinity as articulated by Jesus has its roots in mental science. The Father, The Son and The Holy Spirit are nothing but the super conscious mind and the subconscious mind.

Anything you firmly believe will be your truth. Life is a struggle with our beliefs. Unless you learn to change your beliefs, if they are not harmonious in your life, you are condemned by those beliefs to suffer. On the contrary, the laws of mental science, properly understood and applied, can readily help you to change your beliefs and put you back on the path of peace and harmony as the Creator intended you to enjoy.

CHAPTER SIX

An MBA From the School of Adversity

When I landed in the United States on June 20, 1972, I was enrolled in the School of Adversity, though it was not my school of choice. After having a successful career in Bombay (now Mumbai), India for eight years in the field of teaching and management, the post-Vietnam War American economy could not offer me any suitable job. I went for many interviews for an accounting job or a management job, and almost all of my prospective employers told me without hesitation that my lack of American experience was my handicap. Though I pleaded that I could not gain the experience if not given an opportunity, those pleas fell on deaf ears. As the days went by, I began to feel desperate, desolate, and disillusioned about my job prospects in the land of milk and honey; my dreams began to look like my worst nightmares.

Removed from my family and friends, I came back to my apartment after a few interviews, and felt disgusted about my fate on many days. My good friend, Sri Bajaj, was kind enough to share his apartment with me so that my living expenses were not posing a threat to me. Sri was so kind that he cooked food for me, as I was not in the least trained to make anything in the kitchen except a cup of tea. He took me under his wing, and I tagged along with him to his friend's home, where they all offered good food and friendship. I began to lose my confidence as there were no job prospects looming on my horizon. There were many days that I came home from job interviews and wept for hours, feeling that I had no hope for any job opportunity.

Even though I had teaching experience from India, I was told that I needed, at minimum, a Doctorate Degree to teach under-graduate level classes. I was not found eligible to teach even high school students, as I did not have a teaching license in the United States. I had neither the funds to go back to school, nor was I emotionally prepared to be a student again. Thus I realized to my dismay that my Master's Degree in Accounting from the University of Bombay was of little use in my pursuit of a career in America.

Since I was registered with the Department of Employment Security of the State of Illinois, they sent me for an interview with an Indian attorney who was looking for a person to trans-late life insurance policies for Indian immigrants. I went and met with attorney Mahendra Mehta, who frankly told me that the advertisement was only to file a petition on behalf of one of his clients as was required by the Department of Labor. He was not really looking to hire anybody for that position.

Regardless, he introduced me to his business associate, Mr. Sampath Nama, a brilliant young man who was a couple of years older than me, who was working as an Insurance Executive at that time. Sam, as he was known, was kind enough to talk about the prospects in the insurance business, and he gave me a book I could study in order to take my test for the life insurance license. Since I had nothing to lose and everything to gain, I studied the book and got my life insurance license.

With Sam's help, I was hired as an insurance salesman by the Earl Jordan Agency of Massachusetts Mutual Life Insurance Company, located at 111 West Jackson in Chicago. After I got the license, and some basic training from the agency, I began my career as a life insurance agent in Chicago. Since I did not have any Sales experience, selling insurance did not look very promising.

Since I had a master's degree in accounting, Sam thought that I could help his doctor clients with their income tax returns; he advised me to enroll with H & R Block for their income tax preparation course. Since I did not have any money, he paid $75.00 towards their fee; I was very happy about it as I could learn income tax preparation in this country.

I finished the course by the middle of December, 1972, and I was getting ready for the 1973 tax season. Sam had already told his clients about my availability to do their taxes in the forthcoming season. In the meantime, I sold a life insurance policy for a young physician from India, and my sole income for 1972 was from that sale, which amounted to $600.00.

As the 1973 tax season loomed, I applied to the Income Tax Savers of America, who operated the Montgomery Ward tax store in downtown Chicago. They hired me as a part-time tax return preparer for the Montgomery Ward in Chicago loop. In the meantime, Sam took me as a junior associate, and I began to follow him on his sales interviews to get some experience. I was not going to Montgomery Ward, as the atmosphere was not very encouraging, and the store manager was not very supportive.

One day I got a call from the corporate office, and the gentleman on the other end of the line said, "Mr. Nair, this is Mr. Snyder, vice president of the Income Tax Savers of America home office in Tampa, Florida. We understand that you are a part-time tax return preparer at our State street store. But we do not see you putting any hours there. Is there a reason why you are not going there?"

I was a little rude and said, "Does it make any difference? If I don't go there, you don't pay me."

But the gentleman was really nice, and asked me to explain my reason for no shows.

"Sir, do you want to know the real reason?" I asked him.

"Please, Mr. Nair feel free to tell us."

"I do not like my boss." I blurted.

"We do not like him either," said the vice president. He continued: "Can you take over the store?"

I was dumbfounded. I had not prepared even one tax return in the USA, and I was being offered a job to be the supervisor of a very busy tax store in Chicago. Out of desperation, I said, "Yes, I can."

The vice president and the regional manager flew down to Chicago to meet and have lunch with me. I had a scrumptious lunch at the corporation's expense; the two gentlemen were pleased with me, and they offered me the job. This was the first week of February, and the season got very busy. I had two part-timers to help me. I had a lot of fire in my belly, and I kept on doing most of the tax returns till the store closed. Since I am good with numbers, my lack of experience in completing the tax returns did not intimidate me. During the next seventy days or so, I prepared more than four hundred tax returns by myself, and my average biweekly paycheck was over $500.00. It was a lot of money in 1973.

I was also helping Sam's clients with their tax returns during my spare time, and he was very happy with that. In the meantime, I also found a part-time job with Continental Bank and Trust Company in their mailroom. After I closed the store at Montgomery Ward, I would walk over to the Bank to start my part-time job. It was a night job with a ten-hours shift, and I was paid $2.50 per hour. It was only for three days, and I made an additional $75.00 per week. I knew that the tax season would end in April, and I needed a permanent job. But I could only do the mailroom work for a few weeks as the sleep deprivation was taking a toll on me, even though I was in the prime of my youth.

Since Sam started his own investment company with a group of investors, he offered me a job as the company treasurer. After tax season, my insurance business also started picking up, and my association with Sam really helped me to get out of my despair and lack of confidence. He was indeed a brilliant man, with a vision about his future. I owe him a debt of gratitude for all his help at a time when I was groping in the dark, when my future appeared bleak and dismal.

I left Sam in September 1973 to pursue my own business interest in accounting and tax work. Besides, I was also planning to go to India to get married to my sweetheart there. After six weeks of vacation, I came back from India and started my bookkeeping and tax work in addition to insurance sales. My tax clients were very happy to see me back, and they wanted help in the areas of life insurance and business planning.

My wife came here from India in February of 1974, and we began our life together in Chicago. I took a one-bedroom apartment at 1025 West Hollywood for a monthly rent of $180.00, and it was just enough for the two of us. I continued to sell life insurance for Travelers Insurance Company, as I left the Mass Mutual Agency. I also had a few regular clients for monthly bookkeeping work. Still, I did not have a regular job or a clear career path.

My family began to expand, and I became a father, as our son, Sai, was born. While I was ecstatic about my fatherhood, the burden of additional responsibility was churning new business ideas in my brain. Like any other immigrant, I decided to venture into business and started a travel agency in the first quarter of 1976. The first-generation immigrants kept close ties with their homeland, and I targeted the Indian immigrants' market to sell the airline tickets. My honeymoon with the business began to fade after the first year, as I was confronted with the reality of the marketplace and the looming airline deregulation. I was devoting all my time to work, and the revenue was not enough to meet my monthly expenses of staff salary, rent, telephone, and the like. What seemed to me in 1976 as a boon began to appear as a curse. My dancing dreams began to look like gripping nightmares. My travel agency appeared to me as a black hole, sucking all my financial resources. Since it required my attention in day-to-day management, I was not able to focus on my bookkeeping business. This predicament went on for the next couple of years, drying out my financial resources and my emotional wellbeing.

In the spring of 1980, I made a principal decision to close my business, and to cut my losses and run. By that time, my business was in the red to the tune of $100,000.00. Primarily I owed money to Air India and British Airways who always gave me ticket stocks, without demanding any security deposit from me, so I had a moral responsibility to pay them. I did not consider bankruptcy as an option, as it would inflict a psychological blow to my reputation from which I felt that I would not be able to recover. I made three principal decisions:

1. I would close the business.
2. I would bite the bullet by pooling all my resources, paying off Air India and British Airways.
3. I would not discuss this matter with anybody, including my wife, as she became busier with our second son (who was born towards the end of 1979).

It was a big financial loss for a new immigrant who was in this country for less than ten years, and did not have any full time job. Except for our home, we did not save any money, either.

What did I do wrong? Why did not I succeed in my business, though I put my heart and soul into it? *Maybe I am not cut out to do business—should I go back to my bookkeeping work for my clients?* I asked myself. *What is the secret of success? Why do some people succeed in whatever they do, and many others fail?* These questions started to haunt me day and night.

After I closed my business, I began focusing on my bookkeeping work and life insurance sales. That kept me occupied and provided me with income to meet any household expenses. My mind was still preoccupied with the question *what went wrong?*

What Went Wrong?

Day and night, I asked this question to myself, and my mind was battling unruly thoughts during my waking hours. With an unsettled mind, I was determined to find the answer to my question. I remembered what Socrates, the great Greek philosopher, said: "Know thyself." The great philosopher was an inspiration to me, and I began to read books on self-help, religion, philosophy, and psychology. I began looking for used books, which I could get for a couple of dollars during those days.

I used to go to nearby McDonald's during my spare time, and spend a couple of hours reading those newly-acquired used books. Reading them really helped me to gain a different perspective, and kept inspired at all times. Many of the books I read during that period were the New Age category; this was a new wave of motivational and inspirational material which would help people succeed in their chosen endeavors. Below is a list of books which influenced my quest:

1. *How to Win Friends and Influence People*—Dale Carnegie
2. *Secret of the Ages*—Robert Collier
3. *As a Man Thinketh*—James Allen
4. *Greatest Salesman*—Og Mandino
5. *Holy Bible*
6. *Bhagavad Geetha*
7. *Power of the Subconscious Mind*—Joseph Murphy
8. *Self Mastery Through Auto-Suggestion*—Emile Cue
9. *Power of Positive Thinking*—Norman Vincent Peale
10. *Creative Visualization*—Shakti Gawain
11. *Think and Grow Rich*—Napoleon Hill
12. *Laws of Success*—Napoleon Hill
13. *Acres of Diamonds*—Russell Conwell
14. *Edinburgh Lectures*—Thomas Troward
15. *Law of Psychic Phenomena*—Thomson Hudson
16. *Autobiography of a Yogi*—Paramahansa Yogananda
17. *Positive Mental Attitude*—W.Clement Stone
18. *Creative Process in the Individual*—Thomas Troward
19. *Power of the Spoken Word*—Florence Shinn
20. *Conquest of Happiness*—Bertrand Russell

I have a collection of more than five hundred books in my library, but the books I've listed above are the core books that helped me to recreate my world, and retool my personality. Most of those books I regularly read, and it is correct to say that they are indeed my best friends. I refer to them very often when I am challenged or simply to get a dose of inspiration. It has become my daily routine to read a few pages from any one of those books, when I sip my morning tea. The routine continues even today.

Knowledge Is Useless

Knowledge is utterly useless if it is not applied in everyday life. When I buy a book, I am looking for at least one idea that I can borrow from the book, and then I run with that.

Another thing you can do to stay inspired is to inspire other people. It is said by the wise men and women of the world that the best way to learn is to teach. I am always busy sharing my thoughts and ideas with people around me, and the inspiration I have received from outstanding books and their brilliant authors, I make it a point to share with anybody who is willing to listen. It has given me lot of harmony and peace in my everyday life. Every time I share these ideas of inspiration, it helps me cement my own belief in those pearls of wisdom handed down to us by those giants who preceded us. In teaching we are learning, in sharing we are caring, and in giving we are only receiving. Once you taste the joy of sharing, you will not want it in any other way.

Look for that one idea in every book you read, every lecture you attend, and every tape you hear. For example, when you read the book *Power of Positive Thinking* by Norman Vincent Peale, you'll notice that in the first chapter of the book itself, the author reminds the reader to believe in himself (or herself). Many times, the people who turn out to be having an inferiority complex are those who have actually suffered from the negative suggestions they received from their family, teachers, or friends. They received that limiting belief which was cemented in their consciousness as time marched on. Take this one idea of belief in yourself from the book, and try to practice it in daily life. You can take the following steps in absorbing this idea:

1. Understand and analyze the term "belief."
2. Write down five of your core beliefs.
3. Examine the nature of those beliefs. Are they limiting beliefs or uplifting beliefs? If they are limiting beliefs that have negatively impacted your feeling of self esteem, scrutinize them for their real worth. Like an experienced trial lawyer, interrogate the belief, and remove the veil of falsity understanding the real truth behind the belief.

Look at the following limiting belief: *I need a college education to get a good job*. There is some truth in this belief, as four years of college will help you land a better paying job. It is a very relative statement, but not an absolute one. If you look around in your family or circle of friends, you will find at least a few people who made it without a college degree. Look at their personality traits, and see what they brought to the table to compensate for their lack of college degree. Maybe they started working hard on their job; hard work made them good at what they did and paved their way to forge ahead. Or perhaps they took some courses from the community college to improve their skills, though they did not get a formal diploma. More important than having a diploma is what you do with the knowledge you acquired during your four years of college. Every employer looks at your qualifications when they hire you, as they have nothing else to measure your competency and probability of success. But once you have experience, the employer will want to know how well you accomplished the tasks assigned to you in your previous job. So it is necessary to examine our own limiting beliefs, and interrogate them to bring out the truth in those beliefs, rather than blindly allowing them to be your habitual companion.

Lessons Learned at the School of Adversity

During the last four decades, I learned very valuable lessons from the School of Adversity. I do not think that I would have learned even a fraction of my experience from any university even if I had enrolled in a Ph.D. program. Experience is the best teacher, and the School of Adversity is the best school of learning on earth. So if you go through tough experiences in life, receive it with open arms, as you will be a stronger person, equipped to face the challenges of life, be it in the areas of career, finance, or family relationships.

Nothing is as Easy as it Appears

The first lesson I learned from the School of Adversity is that things are not as easy as they appear at the outset. My great expectation from the travel agency business is living testimony to this. When I started in the travel business, I thought that I had a plan in place, and that it was a good business in which to make money. In less than two years, I realized that I did not do enough market research to assess viability, especially in light of the looming deregulation of travel business by the U.S. government. Besides, I did not have any experience in the business, and therefore I had to rely on other people to get information about the profitability or otherwise of the chosen field. Many times, the information I received was half-baked, rendering it useless for taking costly business decisions. Then there were other factors, like lack of sufficient capital to sustain the business, and the lack of working capital, which limited my ability to have competent help.

The conclusion was that I made an emotional decision to start a business in a field that was unfamiliar to me. The future of this industry itself was threatened with deregulatory rules and regulations, the impact of which was unknown to anyone at that time. If I was a prudent businessman, I would have waited a couple of years to see the impact of deregulation on the survival and profitability of the travel business. My decision to close the business and cut my losses proved to be prudent. Had I not done that, I would have gone deeper in debt, limiting my chances to come out from that financial black hole any time soon. It could have been disastrous, to say the least.

Accept Responsibility for Your Actions

Another important lesson I learned from this episode was the importance of taking full responsibility for one's actions. I accepted full responsibility for the business failure, and did not discuss the matter with anyone. I also learned lessons about assigning blame and focusing on the wrong things. It is not helpful to blame other people, events, or the economy; the blame game only transfers the problem to someone else. It may keep your ego intact, but the problem will still exist.

If you focus on the problem, you are not looking for a solution. Any problem that you allow to fester, either by blame-shifting or through wrong focus, will drain your emotional and mental resources. Once you accept responsibility and give up the blame game, your mental stamina will increase, rendering you able to create solutions.

Help somebody else solve his or her problem; in the process, you will attract a solution to your own problem. I have employed this technique several times, and it has helped me find the solutions I've needed.

Success is a Mindset

Success is a paradigm shift. Your circumstances do not change— you are the same person, but now you look at things differently. When there is despair, you see hope; where there is lethargy you introduce hard work; where there is fear, you instill faith in the goodness of the Universe, or the infinite power.

You can compare your life to a card game: we all get a set of cards from the "dealer," and we must play our cards with diligence in order to succeed. Similarly we all must live and look to be successful in the environment we are in. You do not have to go elsewhere looking for "diamonds," as they are hidden in your own backyard. When there is a paradigm shift, you will be attracting resources that are conducive to your personal success and harmony. The resources that you repelled due to your negativity will start flowing towards you as you have become a psychic magnet, attracting people, conditions, and events necessary to translate your dreams into a physical reality.

This is an invaluable lesson learned in the School of Adversity. During the last three decades, my attitude was always spearheaded by optimism, and an inner feeling that things will work out. Your attitude is the face of your character and it really dictates your altitude in life. An inspired person is like a magnet, its capacity to attract is unmatched. A magnet, it is said, can lift five times its weight when it is charged. But it cannot lift even a feather when it loses the charge.

As emphasized earlier in chapters one and two: a mind that is filled with gratitude alone can invoke more blessings from the Universe. As always, gratitude must be the only attitude.

A Taste of Success

After working and struggling for the last four years, things began to turn the corner. The year was 1984; one of my business associates, an attorney, decided to start a stock brokerage company, and he encouraged me to get my Series Seven (General Securities) license. The new firm sponsored me for the test, and I had no problem getting my stock broker's license.

Though my friend's brokerage firm did not take off due to some technical difficulties, I was able to get my Series Seven license, which was a landmark in my career path. I joined another small brokerage firm, and with my client base, the results were really encouraging. I worked with this firm for two years, and with two years of experience, I was able to move to a medium-sized brokerage firm. By this time, I had become a full-time stock broker, and was very familiar with stock and bonds trade. It was a very exciting time for me, as I always relished new challenges. My production was reasonably good for a newcomer to the industry.

My $10,000.00 Negotiation

I was always looking to move up, and I applied for a broker's position with Dean Witter Reynolds (now Morgan Stanley). I was called for an interview at the Oak Brook office; my prospective boss, Mr. Jerry Reemps, was very pleased with me, and he offered me a job.

It is a custom in the brokerage industry (and financial services industry in general) to offer a guarantee for the first six months by the time the new broker will be able to settle in the new firm. Jerry offered me $4,000.00 per month, and I asked for $6,000.00. Jerry tried to convince me that my production at that time did not make me eligible for the $6,000.00. Since the production was the issue, I told Jerry that I could work for a year and get my production back up before we could meet again. Jerry was agreeable to this.

After a year, in July 1987, I made an appointment with Jerry, who consented to meet with me. The meeting was very cordial; Jerry was pleased with my production numbers and agreed to offer me $6,000.00 a month. I said that I'd been willing to accept $6,000.00 a year earlier—however, I'd waited for that whole year, and there was a cost associated with waiting! Therefore, I asked for $10,000.00 a month guarantee. Jerry almost jumped out of his seat, as he did not expect me to ask for that.

I restated my request in a very amicable way and kept quiet. I read in a book (*Negotiation*, by Steven Cohen) that when you negotiate, you should state your point and "shut up." Whosoever breaks the silence will lose. I wanted to put this principle to test.

Jerry was thinking, and I just sat there with a smile. We might have waited in silence for four or five minutes, and although it felt like a good half an hour, I decided to stick to my understanding of Cohen's rule in negotiation. Finally, Jerry could not take it anymore, and he broke the silence. He argued that $10,000.00 was a lot of money for a fairly new broker. Every time he brought it up, I mentioned the cost of waiting. To make a long story short, Jerry finally agreed, and I walked out of his office with a smile on my face.

I mentally thanked Steven Cohen, whose book I bought for a mere twenty-five dollars a couple of years before my meeting with Jerry Reemps. Indeed the book was worth a hundred times more to me in my negotiation with Jerry. Steven Cohen, I concluded, knew exactly what he was talking about.

Jerry was really happy with me, and I did not disappoint him for the generous offer he made me. I joined Dean Witter in August 1987, and in October 1987 the market crashed (a twenty-two percent drop in DJIA). I was enjoying my $10,000.00 per month salary.

Because of my background in life insurance sales, Jerry made me the Insurance Coordinator for the branch, and I enjoyed that position until I left Dean Witter towards the end of 1989.

A Career with Metlife

Even though I enjoyed the life of a stock broker, I did not want to continue it for the rest of my career due to the tremendous amount of stress involved. It is the nature of the business, and though I was a very calm person, I thought it was not good for me in the long run.

This is the time Mr. Koshy T'Velil, a Branch Manager with Metlife, whom I knew for a couple of years, encouraged me to join Metlife as a full-time agent. Again, I had to negotiate, and Koshy and his boss, Ed Gross, were involved in the negotiation. I mentioned that I was doing well with Dean Witter, and was not planning to make a change, unless they made an offer I could not resist. After a few meetings, Koshy made it clear that he wanted me at any cost, and he was doing the negotiation on my behalf as he was impressed with my sales records.

Finally, they came with a very good offer. Metlife had an MBA recruiting track, where they train fresh MBAs for three and a half years, after which the candidate can choose personal production or management track. I of course did not have an MBA from any school in the United States, but they were able to convince the higher-ups to consider my M.Com from Bombay University in place of an MBA for this purpose. I accepted the position, and it offered a guaranteed salary of $850.00 a week for the next three and a half years. With this base salary, along with my commission income, I was able to make a six-figure income.

First President's Conference

During the first year itself, I qualified for the coveted President's Conference and the prestigious Million Dollar Round Table Conference. I was the first agent to qualify for the President's Conference from Koshy's branch, and that made him extremely happy. We became very close friends, and even after retiring from Metlife, we still maintain a very good friendship.

The President's Conference was held in 1990 at the Princess Hotel in Bermuda. I attended, along with my family. My children (who were fifteen, ten, and six years of age) thoroughly enjoyed the trip. Metlife paid most of the bill, and that made me a happy camper.

My Million Dollar Telephone Call

One day, when I was in the Metlife office in Oak Brook, a telephone call came from Mrs. K, wife of one of my clients. She sounded upset, and she said, "Mr. Nair, I need your help."

"Of course, I can help you, no problem," I assured her.

She had applied for a mortgage loan with a certain mortgage company; she'd left messages, but her loan officer would not return telephone calls. She did not know what to do.

I took the telephone number of the loan officer and the name of the mortgage company, and told Mrs. K that I would do whatever it took to get her the loan. After I finished the conversation, I called the Fortune Mortgage Company and asked for the broker. The young lady told me that he was no longer working there. Then I asked for the owner, and she connected me to one Mr. Joseph Fang. Mr. Joseph Fang was very friendly, and he sent for the file, putting me on hold. He came back and said that the file was almost complete, except for a new pay stub and bank statement. I made an appointment to meet with Joseph next week with the required documents. Mrs. K was very happy, and she furnished the needed documents.

Joseph was a very friendly Chinese gentleman; he immediately took care of the file, and the loan was closed in the next two weeks. Joseph wanted me to meet with him for lunch the next week, and I agreed. I knew Joseph was a very shrewd business-man, and there must have been another agenda he wanted to discuss with me during lunch. After exchanging pleasantries, we set out for lunch in a Chinese restaurant. Joseph told me, to my surprise, "Gopi, if you did work for Mrs. K's file, you might as well get paid for it." In fact, he offered me a job to work with him as a loan officer. I told him that I had a full time job with Metlife, and I could not leave that job. But he wanted me to join him as a part-time loan officer, to which I agreed. He knew my potential, and I recognized the opportunity and seized it. During those days, there was no licensing requirement for mortgage brokers, and the mortgage brokerage business was unregulated.

I continued to work with Joseph til 2002, almost six to seven years. In 2002, I joined Homeland Mortgage Company when Judy Chen started the business. Over the last fifteen to sixteen years, I made over a million dollars in commission. It all began with the call from Mrs. K. The moral of the story is that opportunities appear in disguise as problems. I could have told Mrs. K that I do not do any mortgages, and that I could not help her. She would have understood my position. But I always thought that I was in the problem-solving business. If your client has a problem, you help the client solve it. The only purpose of our business is client service, and the compensation we receive is a byproduct of service. I sincerely believe in this principle.

After seventeen years with Metlife as an Account Executive, Associate Branch Manager, and Branch Manager, I decided to take early retirement from Metlife in 2004. I had a very good career with Metlife, and I qualified during those years for three President's Conferences, several Leader's Conferences, and several Million Dollar Round Table Conferences.

During the last eleven years, I have been working with Mrs. Judy Chen, the President of Homeland Mortgage Company. Judy has been very supportive of me and my sales activities, and that made me very successful in the mortgage business. I could not have achieved this success without the support of Judy, Helen, and Jack Chen, the owners of the company.

CHAPTER SEVEN

Auto-Suggestion— The Ultimate Secret

D uring the last three decades, as I was scanning literature in the fields of self-help, motivation, and success, the most striking thing that I came across is the power of auto suggestion.

We all live in a suggestive world. Some suggestions are explicit, while others are implicit—but all suggestions influence our thoughts, which, based on its intensity, can seep into our subconscious mind, where it is stored in the memory bank. If random suggestions get bogged into our consciousness and influence our thinking, speaking, and acting, why not plant very precise suggestions in the fertile soil of the subconscious mind? Such an act of conscious auto suggestion can produce effects, events, and circumstances to our liking. In other words, we choose the experience we love to have, and plant auto suggestions corresponding to that experience. The following table will shed more practiced light on this vital point:

Experience Desired	Auto-suggestion to be planted
Inner Harmony	Plant auto suggestion of harmony and peace. Example: Every day in every way, I am becoming harmonious. I am grateful for the peace I enjoy.
Success	Plant the auto-suggestion of success. Example: I am grateful for a successful day. I rejoice in my success and in the success of others.
Perfect Health	Plant auto-suggestion of health. Example: I am grateful for the perfect health I enjoy (and pour emotion as you recite).
Straight A's in my school	I am grateful for the straight A's I am getting. <div align="center">OR</div>Every day, in every way, I am improving my grades.

You can custom-craft your own table to fit your particular circumstances. The most important thing to remember is that you decide the experiences (effects) and write them down, while writing down the auto-suggestion (the cause) you need to plant in your subconscious mind.

In the following pages, we acquire in-depth knowledge of the power of auto-suggestion, and a practical way to incorporate this very powerful tool of mind management in your everyday life. The word "impossible" does not exist in the realm of the subconscious—that sleepless giant whose power to manifest desires is indescribable and unmatched. It can attract resources from far and near to translate the dreams of its master (conscious mind) into a physical reality.

Auto-suggestion is a technique available to humankind from time immemorial to induce the subconscious mind. Any external suggestion accepted by an individual knowingly (and most of the time unknowingly) becomes an auto-suggestion. Auto suggestion is a powerful mind management technique, because it has an innate capacity to induce the subconscious mind, that "sleeping giant" who attends to every minute function of the body (all the involuntary functions like respiration, digestion, balancing the chemicals in the body, etc) during the waking and sleeping hours. It is in fact a sleepless giant endowed with stupendous power that, when summoned, can carry out any seemingly impossible task, and the word "impossibility" is not in its dictionary. The only known technique of summoning the power of the subconscious mind is auto suggestion. Almost all of us use this power without the knowledge that we are invoking the power of the subconscious mind. The thoughts we think in the conscious mind, with emotion and passion, seep into the subconscious mind, which executes them with a cunning accuracy. Before we can embark on the power of the subconscious we need to examine the organization human mind.

ORGANIZATION OF THE HUMAN MIND

THINKING MIND
LOGICAL MIND
ARGUING MIND
ACTIVE MIND
MASTER MIND
OBJECTIVE MIND
SEAT OF EGO
INDUCTIVE REASONING

CONSCIOUS MIND

SUBJECTIVE MIND
PASSIVE MIND
OBEYING MIND
ABSORBING MIND
LAW OF BELIEF
DEDUCTIVE REASONING
SEAT OF MEMORY

SUBCONSCIOUS MIND

As mentioned earlier in Chapter Two, within the section titled "How To Cultivate a Grateful Mind," you have only one mind, but based on the fundamentally differing functions, it can be divided into conscious mind and subconscious mind. Each part of the mind is endowed with separate attributes and functions. The conscious mind is the Directing Mind, and can be compared to the captain of the ship, whereas the subconscious can be compared to a loyal and willing servant of the master—the captain. Power of the subconscious mind is matchless, and it is also an inlet into the Universal Mind. Therefore it can draw necessary resources to carry out the master's orders from anywhere in the Universe.

Law of Belief is the Law of the Subconscious. It is based on one of the outstanding attributes of the subconscious mind namely that it works on deductive reasoning. It does not question the order given by the master. Therefore it does not know the difference between any actual experience and a synthetic experience. Hence the saying, "Fake it till you make it." (See Chapter Three, in the section titled "Fake It Till You Make It")

"Whatsoever ye shall pray and ask for, believe ye have received, ye shall receive." This Biblical statement points out the Law of Belief, which is the Law of the Subconscious. Anything that you want to see manifest in life, see it as a present possibility. Visualize your desire as already fulfilled, and it will speed up its manifestation. Thus your desires and dreams must be communicated to the subconscious mind through auto suggestion, and the subconscious will respond in kind by manifesting the desires that you impressed upon it in vivid details. The world without is nothing but a true replica of the world within. If you see disharmony in your life, you ought to go within to check the thoughts lurking in your secret chambers. They are one of disharmony and lack, and as you expel them from your mind, your outside condition will improve. Every thought lodged in your consciousness and accepted by the subconscious is a cause and it will germinate in time to give birth to the corresponding effect. So if the effects (events, circumstances, and conditions) are not of your liking, you cannot change them unless you change the primary cause which was the thought you planted in the soil of the subconscious.

As mentioned in earlier chapters, the subconscious mind is a fertile soil. Every thought is a seed you plant in the fertile soil of the subconscious mind, and it sprouts after its kind to produce the corresponding effect in the thinker. Just like a farmer carefully selects the seeds he wants to sow during the farming season, we all must be carefully selecting the thoughts we think and the words we speak, as they seep into deeper layers of consciousness, where they are converted into events, conditions and circumstances. As the great Master of mind Jesus Christ said "Ye shall know them, by their fruit." It means from the experiences (fruit) you have in life, you can trace back the thoughts (the cause behind the experience).

Another outstanding attribute of the subjective mind is that it is amenable to suggestions. Every suggestion your conscious mind makes, or an external suggestion your conscious mind makes, or an external suggestion picked up by the subconscious when the conscious mind was in a state of abeyance, when accepted becomes an auto suggestion. As we discussed before, the subconscious mind does not compare facts, and arrive at conclusions, as it is incapable of inductive reasoning. Therefore it is imperative that the conscious mind must be "vigilant" at all times to make sure that no unwanted or negative thoughts trespass into the domain of the subconscious. To make the point clear, let us say that you have a new servant at home, who is not familiar with your relatives or friends. If anybody comes to your home in your absence (conscious mind is absent, because it is sleeping), and says he is your friend, the new servant will extend hospitality as though that person was indeed your friend.

This type of dangerous thought intrusion can take place when you watch a violent movie, or pay attention to negative news after dinner or late at night when the conscious mind is in a sleepy state. This is why people who associate with negative people generally turn out to be very negative in their own behavior. Therefore, it is very important for people to watch what they see, hear, or internalize, especially during those vulnerable hours of dawn, dusk and midday. It is equally important for parents to discriminate between positive and negative comments, as the children's innocent mind is like a fertile soil, ready and willing to accept any seeds sown. Encouraging children to associate with friends who are positive and inspiring can also contribute to their healthy emotional growth.

The Subconscious Is The Obeying Mind

Since the nature of the subconscious mind is one of a loyal servant, it does not argue with the conscious mind—the captain of the ship. It does not talk back, or compare facts, like the conscious mind. The roles are clearly defined and there is no gray area. This imposes a greater responsibility on the thinking mind. Thus when you say "I can't do this," "I am getting old," or "I am broke," you are causing harm to the power of the subconscious mind, which simply accepts your comments at face value. It will move the resources necessary to carry out your orders. This an important reason for every person to be careful about what he or she thinks. Henry Ford, the famous industrialist and one of the richest men of all time, had an insight into the power of the subconscious mind when he said:

> "If you think you can do a thing, or think you can't do a thing, you are right."

You must think positively, you must speak inspiring words, and perform non-harmful deeds at all times in order to get the maximum benefits from the invincible power of the subconscious mind. Anything you impress upon the subconscious mind, by induced auto-suggestion, will translate into its physical reality. With pure intentions, noble motives, and sincere prayers, manifestation will speed up itself, as there are no obstacles, impediments or delays in your conscious mind.

Total harmony between the two agencies of human mind is a prerequisite for success and happiness in everyday life. The wisdom of the subconscious mind is readily available to any person regardless of his education, gender, color, religion or race. Armed with the knowledge of the dual function of mind, and recognizing the role of conscious and subconscious mind, anybody can convert failure into success, poverty and lack into prosperity and abundance, and erase fear with hope and optimism. As the great mental scientist Emile Coue recommended, simply repeat the following suggestion in the form of a lullaby at dawn, dusk, or midday:

> "EVERY DAY IN EVERY WAY, I AM GETTING BETTER AND BETTER."

First chant this expression three times aloud, so that you can hear it. The next three times, mutter it like a whisper so that your subconscious mind will be impressed. The third time you say it, do it mentally without moving your lips, and it will be woven into your character.

Your Conscious Mind—Your "Bodyguard"

Your conscious mind is in fact your bodyguard. The language your speak and the thoughts you think are the protective armor around you. As the "captain of your soul," your thinking mind thinks only good thoughts, inspiring thoughts that you give rise to uplifting and equally inspiring words, which attract people of similar thoughts to you. When you have only love, compassion and empathy for others, they too will reciprocate in kind, with similar thoughts and words. Since every dominant thought produces circumstances akin to its innate nature, it is impossible for a person of love and compassion to attract hatred and violence into his life. It is like a farmer sowing the seeds of oranges and getting a harvest of apple. Only oranges can come out of orange seeds, and only apples can come out of the apple seeds.

"Circumstance is a Looking Glass"

As James Allen put it, "Circumstance is a looking glass." It means that you can look through the window of circumstances to your secret chamber of thoughts and impressions. Your events, conditions and circumstances in life are the offspring of your own thoughts, though seldom recognized by man. Just like the giant oak tree is slumbering in a tiny acorn, the mammoth wealth of a great industrialist hides in the simple idea he conceived and nurtured; eventually, he will produce a product using that idea to change the way the world thinks. Google and Facebook stand as indisputable testimony to the above truth.

Whatever you thought in the past made who you are today, and whatever you think today will create your world of tomorrow. But it is tough and almost impossible for an ordinary person to break the old chain of thoughts, and he easily succumbs to his old ways of negativity and fear, blaming his fate for everything.

The power of spoken words is also echoed in Bible, where it is said:

> "Death and life are in the power of the tongue, and those who love it will eat its fruit."

> —Proverbs 18–21

If we examine our speech, it is nothing but movement of spirit. The energy that is stored in us, and is expressed; the expression results in speech. The origin of Divinity was explained in New Testament as follows:

> "In the beginning there was the word, and the word was with God, and the word was God."

> —John 1:1

Thus the word is the ultimate expression of spiritual energy. You can use electric power to light up the whole city, or you can electrocute as many as who touch a "live wire" hanging from a pole in the city. Similarly, you can uplift your conditions in life by using the positive tongue from which only inspiration will roll out. You can also misuse the power of the spoken word (the expression of the ultimate spirit) by using your negative tongue, usually immersed in the pool of negative emotions like lack, poverty, judgment, hate and rivalry.

Many people complain that they are used to negative expression due to family background, or other external influences. Of course habit is a merciless master, and it is a Herculean task to completely get rid of it. Here again, you can consciously choose words that you want to incorporate in your daily conversation. Read a few pages from your scriptures like the Bible, Bhagavad

Geetha, Q'uran, Talmud, etc. and underscore inspiring messages. Those messages invariably contain very inspiring positive words, which you will begin to incorporate in your daily conversation. You can also stop watching movies that contain vulgar language, especially at night when the conscious mind may be slumbering. Another way to improve your positive vocabulary is to daily write down five inspiring words in the English language. An example is given below for ready reference:

May I <u>help</u> you?
I am indeed <u>grateful</u>.
You are so <u>kind</u>.
Your words are <u>inspiring</u>.
I <u>trust</u> you.
Your <u>faith</u> is <u>strong</u>.

The above exercise may appear to be small and simple. But there are no big things in life—only small things that make a big difference. Just like the Chinese say, "A journey of a thousand miles begins with a single step." By taking these baby steps, you will learn to walk on the royal path of inspiration and optimism. A small dose of inspiration a day will provide the essential nutrients for your spirit, to make you a strong person ready to meet daily challenges.

How to Attract Wealth with Auto-Suggestion

"As above, so below
As within, so without."

The above words represent the ultimate secret of creation: the wisdom of the ancients, and the principle of manifestation. As above (in heaven, or spirit), so below (on earth, or in physical form). Thus anything you want to manifest in your life, including wealth, must be borne out of a burning desire—a deep-rooted desire to manifest, possess and enjoy every form of wealth. Such a desire can be created by consciously thinking about it until those thoughts become your dominant thoughts. Dominant thoughts attract similar thoughts, following the Law of Attraction, capable of facilitating events, conditions and experience for the production of wealth.

> "Mind is the Master—power that molds and makes,
> And Man is Mind, and evermore he takes,
> The Tool of Thought, and, shaping what he wills,
> Brings forth a thousand joys, a thousand ills—
> He thinks in secret, and it comes to pass:
> Environment is but his looking glass."
>
> —James Allen

Thoughts constitute mental energy, spiraling bits of electrons and protons, moving at the speed of an electric train. But this energy has no form (unappropriated energy) and it has no direction. When you think about wealth, the word *wealth* followed. Your power of imagination started creating the spiritual prototypes of different forms of wealth, whether it be in the form of money, a home, an automobile, a factory, or anything else. Thus every form of wealth you see in this world is made by somebody's imagination—the most Godlike quality in man. There is a Directing Intelligence behind any form of matter, which is condensation of pure energy.

In man, the Directing Intelligence is the conscious mind, the logical mind, the Master Mind which is the seat of ego. As the Gospel of St. John explains,"In the beginning there was the word. And the word was with God. And the word was God." A word is the verbal expression of a Thought Image, which is the seed of every creation. Thus every creation has to be preceded by a corresponding mental image. Just like a tiny seed of an acorn contains the potential of a gigantic oak tree, so also the small word—*wealth*—is filled with potential to amass any kind of wealth in any amount. The word *wealth* represents potential wealth, which is anything of value that we want to possess. We human beings are endowed with this Directing Intelligence, known as conscious mind, and the degree of its development in each of us is based on the depth of belief in its power, and its use to produce the wealth desired.

Intensity of Purpose

"Let there be light" commanded God, the creator, the architect of the Universe. Since you are made in the image and likeness of God, you are endowed with the same power—power of selection and choice. All of us use this power of creation and the power of selection in our everyday life. Most of us are not happy and contented with the world we create, but we do possess the process of creation, and we are creating a world, even if it does not appear to be a world of our liking. If the farmer does not like the harvest he received, he does not curse the harvest; instead, he changes the seeds he will sow. Similarly, if we do not like our world—which is the result of our thoughts—then we must go back to our thoughts and change them. The subconscious has acted upon your command (your thoughts) and created a world correspondent to those thoughts.

Alter Your Thoughts, Alter Your World

If you are poor, or do not have a well-paying job, you can change your conditions by altering your thoughts. This is a three step process:

1. Write down your dominant thoughts.
2. Replace them with thoughts of wealth and abundance.
3. Change your friends and family if associates if necessary.

Dominant Thoughts of a Poor Person

1. I am a victim of the society.

2. Rich people and business people exploit the poor.
3. I don't have even a high school diploma.
4. I am not smart, because I do not have a high school diploma.
5. I am a failure, it is my fate.
6. Government is not doing enough for us—we need more food stamps, and more public aid.
7. America is doomed.

If you look at the above seven thoughts, you will see that there are recurring themes binding them: blame, and lack of hope. There is also the absence of one common thought—personal responsibility.

No problem can be solved unless you take personal responsibility for your current situation. It is also true that you cannot solve a problem if your focus is on the problem. Instead, you think away from the problem—think about the solution: The more you think about the problem, more negativity will creep into your thought process, and the blame game begins, expending your energy. The subconscious mind, acting upon the master's command (the dominant negative thoughts), produce more of the same. And the problem becomes deeper and deeper with no solution in sight. When someone asks you, you say "Same old, same old..."

Replacing Thoughts—With Wealth and Abundance

1. I am grateful for the wealth I have.
2. I am grateful for the home we have.
3. I am grateful for the cars we have.
4. I am grateful for the freedom and peace I have with wealth.
5. I am grateful for the knowledge I have for creating wealth.
6. I am grateful for the wealth consciousness arising in me.
7. I am grateful for the awareness that wealth is good for the uplifting of mankind.

Wealth Creating Rituals

1. Release money with joy, and it will come back to you multiplied.
2. Show respect towards any form of wealth, cash, checks, automobiles, homes, etc. which represents wealth in its physical form.
3. Write checks with joy, even when it is for a parking ticket, or a traffic ticket (Affirm "I am grateful for the lesson.").
4. Show generosity in small matters—for example, if you give two-dollar tip for a personal service, increase it to three, and from three to four, etc.
5. Being wealthy is a mindset; always think of the good things money can do.
6. Avoid using the expressions, "I am broke," "I have no money," etc. Instead, always remain grateful when talking about money, and dealing with any form of wealth.
7. Never think of taking advantage of another person when you are negotiating to buy a home, a car, furniture, etc.
8. Always insist on the salesman making a reasonable commission for his services.
9. If you see a "homeless person," give him five or ten dollars with love. Never make any negative comment about his "predicament."
10. Wish for others what you wish for yourself. Do not feel envy towards anyone in their success and prosperity.

If you look at wealthy individuals, you will see that they are the champions of charity. They use part of their wealth for common good, often to help the underprivileged and weaker sections of society. They set up endowments and scholarships in schools and other educational institutions. In short, they release money with joy, and it comes back multiplied.

The Greatest Charity

The Bill and Melinda Gates Foundation is the richest charity in the world. The Foundation has assets worth over thirty-six billion dollars, and both Bill and Melinda are committed to making a positive change in the health and wellbeing of people, particularly in developing countries. They both travel to many countries, focus on preventing needless deaths caused by lack of vaccines, and encourage families to use contraceptives to limit deaths of young women in childbirth. Their personal interaction with those underprivileged men, women and children stand as testimony to their personal commitment to change the world for the better. They are two caring individuals who want to share their wealth with the world so that it will be a better place to live for millions of people who have no chance otherwise to improve their living conditions.

It is no accident that Bill Gates, the founder of Microsoft, is the second richest man in the world, with assets worth over sixty-one billion dollars. If we all can learn one thing from Bill and Melinda Gates, it is that we can make a difference by helping our fellow human beings. You do not have to be a billionaire or even a millionaire to open your wallet for the needy brothers and sisters who share the planet with you. You do not have to travel to third world countries to extend a helping hand. You can find opportunities in your own backyard, or you can help the local food pantry or the soup kitchen who feed the thousands who remain hungry otherwise. It is the birthright of every human being, wherever they are, to eat at least couple of times a day; it is the moral responsibility of every one of us to make sure that we pitch in to promote the cause.

As written in the New Testament: "Whoever has will be given more, and they will have an abundance." In the Biblical story of the talents, those servants who doubled their talents for their master were given more and were invited to partake in the happiness of the master. And the one servant who did not do anything with the talent given to him was punished by losing what was given to him.

Wealth is something to be shared so that it can multiply; that which is hoarded and withheld will eventually wither away. A part of your wealth (even if it is only a couple of dollars) must be set aside and given to charity.

The secret of increasing wealth by giving is enshrined in the very Law of the Universe:

"UNIVERSE RECIPROCATES IN KIND—MANIFOLD."

Almost all the wealthy people know this secret, and they have all opened their wallet to support various humanitarian needs around the world. One of the richest men the world has ever known—namely John D. Rockefeller—knew the secret of increasing wealth by giving at the very tender age of sixteen. Even though he was making a meager amount of fifty cents a day, he used to set aside a part of it for saving, and another part for charities.

The Science of Getting Rich

The Science of Getting Rich is a classic in the field of new age psychology and self help literature, written by Wallace D. Wattles. He has extensively described the spiritual aspect of material accomplishing, especially relating to the art of getting rich. The fundamental truths about getting rich is nothing but a paradigm shift, a mental make-up, an attitude of abundance in everything, and a rearrangement of one's thoughts as they are anchored in wealth consciousness. You can cultivate wealth consciousness by carefully choosing the thoughts that induce wealth and abundance in place of poverty and lack. Just like a farmer who decides to reap a harvest of wheat and carefully selects the healthy wheat seeds to sow in the prepared field, you too can select thoughts of abundance and wealth in the fertile soil of the subconscious mind. It is the receptive mind, and it acts on any command given by the conscious mind.

Tree of Abundance

Thoughts of abundance and wealth which we consciously think about become manifested in due course as wealth in different forms. Thinking thoughts and creating effects (of abundance or lack of it) is going on in every human mind. Most of us experience lack because our mind is constantly entertaining the fear of lack and limitation. The moment we change our thoughts, we are on the royal path of abundance and plenty. Rich people surround themselves with rich people and various forms of wealth; they engage in conversation with their friends about wealth production; they release funds to make a difference in the lives of less fortunate ones. Their minds constantly swim in the ocean of wealth consciousness, and because they sow the seeds of wealth, they harvest wealth in different forms throughout their life.

Wealth is Your Birthright

Wealth is your birthright. Demand it by first choosing thoughts of wealth and abundance. Surround yourself with people who are wealthy, or at least go to the library and read the biographies of Andrew Carnegie, J.P. Morgan, Henry Ford, John D. Rockefeller, Bill Gates, Warren Buffett and other self-made billionaires who started their lives in humble surroundings. They knew exactly what they wanted. Their thoughts were focused, and they backed it up with sheer hard work and ceaseless optimism. That does not mean that they did not face challenges; they did, just like you and me, but their determination to succeed was too strong to be defeated by any undercurrents of adversity.

Think Big

Most of us settle for less and underestimate our potential. The following poem should awaken in us an urge to ask for more from life, who is a "just employer."

> "I bargained with life for a penny
> And life would pay no more,
> However I begged at evening
> When I counted my scanty store.
> For life is a just employer;
> He gives you what you ask,
> But once you have set the wages,
> Why you must bear the task.
> I worked for a menial's hire
> Only to learn, dismayed,
> That any wage I have asked of Life,
> Life would have paid."

—Jessie B. Rittenhouse
"The Door of Dreams"

How to Think Big?

This is a four-step process.

#1   KNOW WHAT YOU WANT. For example, I want a beautiful white brick home.

#2   Formulate the thought of a beautiful white brick home.

#3   Register and hold the thought in your mind. The best way to accomplish this is to see the picture of your beautiful white brick home with your inner eyes. (Mentally visualize the picture of your beautiful white brick home).

#4   Relax and let go. This step is a very important one to practice. When you relax and let go, you are not worrying about the way your desire is going to manifest. This is the time negative thoughts could creep into your domain of consciousness. You will start doubting your ability to manifest your beautiful white brick home. If that happens, you simply state: "I am grateful for the lesson."

How I Manifested My White Brick Home

I personally went through the process in 1989 when I manifested my desire of having a beautiful two-storey white brick house. Our old house was getting smaller as our three boys were growing big, and we started looking for the home. Since my wife wanted to live only in Elmhurst, we were looking for a house on the South side of Elmhurst. I was driving around on my way home one day and saw a beautiful house for sale on the South side of Elmhurst. I suddenly fell in love with the house as it was a beautiful white brick home, two stories, of course. I told my wife, and we went for an open house that weekend. My wife also liked the house as it had five bedrooms, two and a half bathrooms, a big basement, and a big backyard for the kids to play in.

There was only one problem: we were planning to go to India the next week to celebrate my mother's eighty-fourth birthday. It is a big celebration in Indian culture, as a person is said to have seen one thousand full moons when she turns eighty-four. We were all excited about the trip, and I told my wife that if it was meant for us, and we would have it.

Over the next few days, we remained in town, and I went on my ritual, which was to drive around the house in the morning on my way to work and in the evening on my way back. Before we left for India, I must have driven around the house more than a dozen times, and the picture of this beautiful house was implanted in my inner consciousness. I visualized the home in minute detail; the Italian marble in the foyer was a point of attraction for me. I was also thrilled to have a first-floor office room for myself with lots of book shelves. With all the enchanting details in my mind, I was able to visualize the home, day and night.

We went to India for six weeks and came back just in time for the school opening for the kids. The same day we landed in Chicago, I went to see the house from outside. I was slightly disappointed as the "For Sale" sign was gone. *Maybe it was sold*, I thought. But I was so attached to the house that I decided to call the owner whose telephone number I had. His name was Mr. Frank. He told me that he did not get any reasonable offers, and he took it off the market. I heaved a sigh of relief, and told him of my interest in the house. He was also very happy that I was interested. After discussing with my wife, I met with Mr. Frank during the Labor Day weekend and made an offer he could not resist. He looked at his wife for consent, and she nodded, signaling her agreement. There was no real estate agent involved in the transaction, which was the main reason why it was very attractive to the Frank family.

Even though I had similar experiences in the past, this was a major event involving our primary home. This experience only confirmed my belief that our desires are manifested first on the mental plane, then descending onto the physical plane. My falling in love with the home at first sight was my spiritual acceptance of the home, and my constant visits and visualization expedited acceptance by the subconscious mind. Even though there was a gap of almost two months, my desire was deep and emotionally charged for "my dream home." The subconscious mind orchestrated all the events that led to the withdrawal of the home from the market by the owners. This is clear evidence that the power of the subconscious mind to carry out its command with a cunning accuracy cannot be underestimated. When I left for India, I had no trace of fear that I might not get the house. I was confident that if this home was meant for us, nobody could take it away from us.

There was also another factor that led to the consummation of this real estate transaction. I did not take any unfair advantage of Mr. Frank's situation, as I offered a very reasonable price, which, coupled with the absence of any realtor, made his financial situation better by accepting my offer.

We also told the Frank family to take whatever appliances or other personal property he chose; they were very grateful for our gesture of goodwill.

Obstacles to Wealth Accumulation

Let us look at Mother Nature. She is profoundly wealthy, and abundance is her calling card. Wherever we look there is prosperity and wealth. Similarly, if we take mankind as a whole, collectively we have immeasurable wealth; it is spread in all the seven continents, and as we progressed during the last one hundred years, we collectively accumulated more than our previous generations put together. Every generation becomes more aware of the need for wealth accumulation, and due to better economic conditions, they are able to put aside more than their previous generation.

While the race is rich, and the average individual is poor, and there must be a reason for that gap in wealth accumulation. The reason for this predicament of the individual in his inability to create wealth, which can be traced back to his own state of mind. If the thoughts that the individual entertains are but of lack and limitations, the corresponding conditions will manifest in his own personal life.

Dominant Thoughts Are Anti-Wealth Creations

Our thoughts are influenced by our family, society, teachers and others who could have been directly or indirectly associated with our mental development. Many people misinterpret the

Scripture and say that money is the "root" of all evil. Scripture says that it is the love for money (to the exclusion of everything else) is the root of all evil. Money is indeed good as long as it brings joy to others. But if you accumulate it only to hoard and not to give away for those in need, it could lead to evil thoughts and actions, which could lead one to his financial ruin.

Thus if you have been misinformed about what Scripture says about money, that it is the root of all evils, now you can correctly interpret it to say that, "Money is good, as long as it brings joy to others."

From today onwards, watch your thoughts to make sure that they are not those of anti-wealth accumulation. You can look at money as a means to an end—it could be for food, clothing or shelter. It could also be used to make positive changes in the lives of others. In your conversation with others, think positively about wealth in general and do not condemn any form of wealth. You must shun any negative thoughts or speech about anything in life. Any negativity, either in trait or behavior or environment, when discussed and thus relived, will take strong roots in your consciousness and become a part of your own personality. Always remember that your present life is nothing but the harvest of yesterday's thoughts. If you do not like what you see in your life today, you will have to alter the thoughts that went into the making of today.

Negative Imagination

Another obstacle to wealth accumulation is the imagination of lack, poverty, and fear. Many of us are the victims of negative imagination, which is either genetically transferred or acquired from association with friends or family members who habitually think negatively. The aphorism, "What I have feared has fallen upon me" is a very true statement as it invites fear thoughts to manifest as your experience in life. Every negative thought, as soon as it creeps up, can be converted into its positive counterpart.

For example, if you are afraid of losing your job, and as the imagination paints the details of your fear and anxiety, just say loudly, "I am grateful for the lesson." If one of your associates at work got laid off, rather than talking about the employment policy of your employer, just comfort your associate by saying that "when one door closes, seven doors open. Maybe the good Lord has a better plan for you." Rather than leading a conversation stemming from negativity, you can lead your associate to an inspirational path of optimism and expectation. If you can send his résumé to a few of your friends for consideration, that will be ideal. That is what being a good friend is all about.

Ignorance of the Source of Supply

The source of all wealth is spirit—unappropriated spirit. You are surrounded by the sea of unappropriated spirit, and God the creator, your own higher potential, has given you the tools to convert the unappropriated spirit (energy) into appropriated energy in any form you choose to have. Thus wealth in any of its forms is your fruit for the asking, once you know how to ask. "Ask you shall receive, seek you shall find. Knock, it shall be opened unto you." This is not a religious statement; it is in fact a metaphysical truth expressed in simple words.

You have to shake off the thoughts of lack, limitation and poverty. Instead, fill your mind with thoughts of plenty, abundance and wealth. Every thought is pregnant with invisible power capable of transforming the unappropriated spirit into any form you choose to visualize. As explained in *The Science of Getting Rich*:

> THOUGHT is the only power which can produce tangible riches from the Formless Substance. The stuff from which all things are made is a substance

which thinks, and a thought of form in this substance produces the form.

Here, thought does not mean a random thought that flees the mind after a short visit. A strong thought, a dominating thought with fervent emotion, becomes a command to the subconscious mind to act and create a corresponding form, and it simply obeys the master.

No thought of form can be impressed upon original substance without causing the creation of the form.

"What Have You Got in the House?"

There was a crowd of people who followed Jesus for three days, and they were weary and tired as they had not eaten anything. The disciples were puzzled because they had hardly anything enough to feed the thousands of men, women and children.

"How many loaves have ye?" Jesus asked them. Jesus took those seven loaves and gave thanks and broke them. Then He gave to the disciples to set them before the multitude to eat. There were a couple of pieces of fish, too. Jesus blessed that, and commanded the disciples to put them before the people. All of them ate and were filled, leaving a few pieces in the basket.

In this miraculous feeding of the multitude, there hides a spiritual principle. "Anything you have, even if it is so little, if you bless it, and express your gratitude, it will swell and multiply." This is the Law of Increase.

You can apply this spiritual principle in your task of building wealth. Even if you have no significant amount of money, you express gratitude for what you have and bless that form of wealth. Release it with joy for a common good; it will come back to you multiplied. When you do this, have an unshaken faith in this principle and patiently wait, expressing gratitude for fortunes to materialize in your life.

The Law of Increase says:

> I am success, though hungry, cold, ill clad,
> I wander for awhile, I smile and say,
> It is but for a time, I shall be glad
> Tomorrow, for good fortune comes my way,
> God is my Father, He has wealth untold,
> His wealth is mine—health, happiness and gold.

—Ella Wheeler Wilcox

Whatever is praised and blessed multiples. This is the eternal Law of Increase. It does not matter what your financial situation is and how much deeply in debt you are; if you practice this Law of Increasing Returns, you will invite good fortunes into your life. Your emotional prayer will cause the unappropriated energy (this is the spiritual energy that belongs to none—a spiritual no-man's land) to move, causing the formation of wealth you desire.

It may not necessarily mean that somebody is going to transfer money into your bank account. Instead, a friend of yours could suggest you to apply for a position in his company, and the paycheck from that employer could be a direct transfer into your bank account. However miniscule they may appear to be, do not let opportunities pass by.

Our advancement as the entire human race has taught us one very important lesson: nature obeys us in exact proportion to our own obedience to nature. This Law is equally applicable to us in the field of building wealth. We need to respect wealth, obeying the principles of wealth creation; we not worry about being wealthy, as the flow of wealth towards us becomes imminent. When we study the lives of the richest people in the world, one thing is for sure—they all revere wealth; they adore wealth; and they use it for the benefit of mankind. In short, they release wealth with joy, and it surely comes back multiplied!

"Assume A Virtue, If You Have It Not" (Shakespeare)

This is a very wonderful Mental Science principle. You can very well use it in being rich. When you fill your mind with thoughts of wealth, you begin the journey towards riches. It is a single step any aspiring wealthy person can take. Register the thought of being rich and hold it in your mind until the message is picked up by the subconscious mind, which will act on it to convert your desire into a physical reality. You can take the following steps to assume the virtue of being rich:

1. **THINK LIKE A RICH PERSON**

First and foremost, a rich person reveres and respect money. Do not throw a dollar bill like a piece of garbage. When you come home, if you have any change in your pocket, please put it in a coin jar, and never throw it. Even the smallest denomination of a coin—like a penny—is representative of wealth. Even when you talk about money, say good things, and remain grateful.

Similarly, when you write a check for any reason, release it with joy, even if you are writing a check to the Internal Revenue Service or the State Department of Revenue. Anything you release with respect will come back to you, many times multiplied.

Another important characteristic of a rich person is that he honors his financial commitments and pay the bills on time. Paying your bills on time is respect to the other person who has to fulfill his financial commitments from the funds you transfer. It is also true that a good percentage of your credit score (thirty-thirty-five percent) is based on your on-time payment of your financial obligations. Such on-time payments will enhance your credit score, which is a barometer of credit worthiness in the lending world.

2. DRESS LIKE A RICH PERSON

You do not have to go and buy a $600.00 or $1000.00 suit to dress like a rich person. Depending upon your dress code at work, simply wear clean, pressed clothes. Wearing good clothes also positively impacts your mental attitude. Your personal demeanor should be one that is inspiring and uplifting rather than promoting a negative feeling of depression.

3. SPEAK LIKE A RICH PERSON

"Richness" does not only mean material wealth, it also denotes spiritual wealth. The soothing and inspiring words you speak promote spiritual wellbeing in your friends and associates. Anybody can use an inspiring expression to feel good about himself or herself. The best way to stay inspired is by inspiring others.

4. ACT LIKE A RICH PERSON

Most rich people are very humble, and humility is one of their outstanding personality traits—especially when they are dealing with their personal staff; ideally, they often show more compassion and empathy. Their wealth has not inflated their ego; rather, it has only made them very caring human beings. There are always exceptions to the general rule, but we are not talking about those exceptions. You act the way you want to act when you become rich.

If you think like a rich man, speak like a rich man, dress like a rich man, and act like a rich man, then you are already a rich man. You must be rich in your own mind first before you appear before the world as a rich and successful person.

www.ingramcontent.com/pod-product-compliance
Lightning Source LLC
Chambersburg PA
CBHW030308130626
46549CB00002B/752